TOON UP!

by J. J. Gammond

G2 entertainment

Published by G2 Entertainment Ltd

© G2 Entertainment 2017

ISBN: 978-1-782-81-7383

AUTHOR: Jules Gammond

PUBLISHERS: Edward Adams and Jules Gammond

PICTURES: Action Images

PRINTED IN EUROPE

SPECIAL THANKS TO:
Stan Anderson for providing the foreword.

DEDICATED TO:
Cecil Grundy, part of Newcastle United's record attendance of 68,386 in September 1930.

CONTENTS

Stan Anderson leads out Newcastle United for his first match, at home to Cardiff City on 9 November 1963.

Manager Joe Harvey, director Lord Westwood and captain Stan Anderson with the second division trophy, 29 May 1965.

England international Stan Anderson is the only man to captain, Newcastle United, Sunderland and Middlesbrough. A cultured player brought to Tyneside by Joe Harvey, Stan missed just one game as he led Newcastle to promotion a year before England became World Champions. Now living in Doncaster, in his eighties and still a regular golfer, United's promotion has brought a big smile to Stan who after managing and coaching at home and abroad worked as a scout for Newcastle in the late eighties and early nineties.

I'm as delighted as anyone to see Newcastle United make an immediate return to the Premier League. Under the guidance of Rafa Benitez, Newcastle have made that achievement look straight forward, but that is not the case.

When a club of Newcastle's stature appear in the Championship everyone wants to raise their game against them which makes it difficult to get the results needed over a long season. However after a difficult beginning Newcastle have always looked destined for an immediate return and hopefully better days ahead.

Four years after I captained Newcastle to promotion in 1965 the club won a European trophy. With Benitez's experience Newcastle now need to back him and take the club on to the kind of success that seemed possible during the Keegan years. Success in the north-east has been far too thin on the ground in my life-time and so it is heartening to see Newcastle back where they belong and I hope that in the years to come more silverware will arrive at St. James' Park as a reward to the supporters who have stuck with them so well and for so long.

STAN ANDERSON

Captain of Newcastle's 1964/65 promotion winners

No-one wanted to be in the Championship but once you're there you have to get out of it as quickly as possible. Had Rafa Benitez not decided to stay at St. James,' Newcastle United may well be contemplating another season in the second tier rather than an instant return to the top flight.

Next time round in the Premier League, under the guidance of Benitez there is every reason to hope that United will once again soon be able to count their place in the table from the top of it rather than from the bottom. Benitez isn't at Newcastle to be an also-ran. The man is a winner and winning became a regular feeling under Rafa as he took the Toon Up.

Only twice was a win a solitary one. Victories over Forest to close 2016 and Villa in February stood alone, surrounded by defeats at the turn of the year and draws in February. Otherwise when wins came, they came in packs under Benitez. Excluding cup ties, runs of five, eight, three, two, two, two and three meant that Newcastle succeeded in stringing results together, the runs in the first half of the season paving the way back to the Premier League.

On the road United reigned supreme, setting a club record 14 away wins, winning four more points than any other club (Fulham) and conceding six fewer goals than the second best defence (Sheffield Wednesday). There were even more wins at home, 15 of them, with exactly a goal per game conceded at St. James' while home fans witnessed fractionally fewer than two goals for per match

Newcastle's consistency saw them take just two points fewer away than at home. In comparison runners' up Brighton relied more on home form, where they collected 15 more points than they managed on their travels.

Rafa called on 30 players to appear in the Championship, Paul Dummett missing just one game, while Jamaal Lascelles and the dynamic duo of Jonjo Shelvey and Matt Ritchie also topped 40 games.

In total 100 goals were scored in league and cup, Dwight Gayle top scoring in the league with 23 with Ritchie also in double figures with a dozen in the championship.

It was a season to remember as more than a million spectators came through the St. James' turnstiles to grab a piece of the action and see The Toon prove they were simply the best in the league.

Leagues are won with routine bread and butter wins. Narrow victories against the likes of Wigan and Burton don't earn any fewer points than bigger or more dramatic score-lines and there were plenty of the latter.

Newcastle made the rest of the country sit up and take notice when a stunning 6-0 away win at Queens Park Rangers lifted them into an automatic promotion place for the first time on the back of a fifth successive league triumph.

Shortly afterwards there was even more excitement as a sensational fight-back from a 1-3 deficit at home to Norwich dramatically turned into a last gasp victory after two injury time goals.

Poor Preston really copped it, as in addition to being beaten on their own patch they conceded 10 goals on two trips to Tyneside. Slaughtered 6-0 in the League Cup they had another four put past them on the night United secured promotion.

Title rivals Brighton had an expert in charge: the always popular Chris Hughton who had led Newcastle to the championship title in 2010. Hughton's Seagulls took Rafa's Magpies all the way. The two clubs made it into the top two by October. From then on no-other club broke into the automatic places as United and Albion alternated top spot in a battle that would go right down to the final minute of a long, long season until United finally emerged as champions.

Toon Up takes you on a journey of a season to remember. Every game and every goal is covered as the story of the season unfolds with Rafa's reflections and the games put into context.

The Rafalution would never have happened without The Toon Army whose show of support as 'Rafa Remainers' convinced the former Real Madrid manager to stick with this special club in the Championship.

Rafa recruited a squad ready for all that the championship could throw at them. Benitez cut his cloth accordingly, filling it with players experienced at the level they'd be playing at, having jettisoned some on superstar wages but who mightn't have fancied being asked to turn out at The Pirelli Stadium or Griffin Park.

Thanks to Benitez the 2017-18 will see United back in with the big boys and with Rafa recognising The Toon Army's passion for long overdue success, with luck it might be a case that there is more to come and that as long as Rafa is the Gaffer the Toon will stay on the up.

CHAPTER 1

SPURRED ON

Benitez came too late to stop the drop. March 11th 2015 was the turning point for the club. Steve McClaren was sacked with Rafael Benitez appointed to the Toon hot-seat on the same day.

The damage had been done. United lay one off the bottom of the table and had lost their last three games badly. Beginning with a 5-1 trouncing at Chelsea, there had been a dismal single goal reverse at Stoke before Bournemouth had come to St. James' and handed out a football lesson in winning 3-1.

Benitez was thrown in at the deep end with a visit to a Leicester side en-route for the Premier League title although an improved performance resulted in a narrow 1-0 defeat.

Heartened by that Rafa was unveiled to the Geordie Nation before a home derby with Sunderland where Aleksandar Mitrovic began the Rafalution with the first goal of Rafa's reign to take a point.

Defeats followed at relegation rivals Norwich City as well as at Southampton before Benitez began to produce results. None of the final six games would be lost as United scrapped for survival but unfortunately it was too little too late after a wasteful campaign.

While the disappointment at going down for the second time in eight seasons ran deep it was clear that at long last Newcastle had the right man in charge. The question was: now that they'd found him, could they keep him?

A handsome 3-0 win over Swansea was full of positive signs before a creditable draw at home to Manchester City who had walloped United 6-1 at The Etihad earlier in the season. Better still was to come as Newcastle negotiated difficult fixtures, the next one against Liverpool at Anfield.

With Jurgen Klopp's men chasing European qualification it was a tough assignment for Rafa on his return to the Reds, and it looked tougher when the troops came into the visiting dressing room at half time 2-0 down. Benitez got into them though. Being two or more down didn't mean a Benitez team were beaten – as he'd proved in his own time with Liverpool.

Almost straight after the re-start United were back in the game through a header from Papiss Cisse and then half way through the second period The Magpies were level through Jack Colback as The Toon spiritedly secured their first away point of 2016. Under Benitez the away form would become as tremendous as it had been terrible before he arrived.

Hope erupted as Alan Pardew's Palace were defeated the following Saturday at St. James' courtesy of the only goal of the game by ultimately Palace bound Andros Townsend while Karl Darlow matched his heroics by saving Yohan Cabaye's penalty leaving Pards to Pontificate, "For long periods we looked in control of the game" adding, "I thought the reception I got was muted, which was nice. A lot of people understand that I managed here to the best of my ability and we had some good times that I lean on."

Under new boss Benitez there were good times to come, but still short-term difficulties to face. The penultimate fixture took United to doomed Aston Villa who had long since been relegated and had only half as many points as Newcastle, so marooned were they at the foot of the table. Villa Park had bad memories for the Toon Army of course and the home fans were in up in arms about the state of their club, halting the match at one point with a synchronised hurling of beach balls onto the pitch.

Chances came for Newcastle but the breakthrough didn't. A goalless draw proved costly and by the time United took to the field again results elsewhere meant they were already condemned to the drop despite being unbeaten in five games as Rafa tried to turn the tide.

For the final home fixture of the six season stay in the Premier League Newcastle welcomed Tottenham Hotspur. Under Mauricio Pochettino Spurs had become one of the most exciting sides in the land.

For months they had looked like the team most likely to snatch the Premier League crown if surprise package Leicester hit a long awaited bad run and slipped up. In an extraordinary season The Foxes succeeded in out-running the chasing pack leaving Tottenham with the expected consolation of the runners' up place and with it a first finish above their local rivals Arsenal in over two decades. A point would guarantee that for Spurs while with nothing to play for there was a fear that Newcastle would succumb to a Spurs side whose free-flowing football had made them the darlings of so much of the media.

However this was after all St. James' Park, a place where usually the only thing that can be expected is the unexpected. If he was going to go, Benitez wanted to go with a bang. To every last man, woman and child, the Toon Army were determined to do everything in their power to convince the manager that this was the place he should continue to call home. Newcastle might be down but over 50,000 turned up, not so much to see an already relegated team but to persuade the manager to stay.

This was no end of season kick-a-bout. Tottenham wanted to win and were one of the best teams in the land but were swept away on a Tyneside tidal wave. The soon to depart Gini Wijnaldum put United ahead with Aleksandar Mitrovic doubling the lead but it all seemed too good to be true.

Sure enough Spurs pulled one back on the hour through Erik Lamela and when Mitrovic got himself sent off a few minutes later the game had all the makings of one where having got into a winning position, Newcastle would throw points away.

Moussa Sissoko's next game in the Premier League would be for Tottenham rather than against them and while his value soared after an impressive European Championship in the summer, he didn't do himself – or United's bank balance – any harm here. Before Pochettino's pretenders could take advantage of United being a man down Sissoko showed how powerful a presence he could be by surging into the visitors' box and being brought down for a penalty.

Wijnaldum promptly added to his own value by converting the spot-kick for his second of the game as 10-man Newcastle re-established a two goal lead. With the Toon Army's emotional songs in Rafa's praise tumbling down from the stands above, Champions League qualifiers Spurs simply melted away.

Incredibly a side who had never lost by more than one goal in the Premier League all season suddenly leaked two more to a team heading for the Championship rather than the Champions League. Late goals from Rolando Aarons and Daryl Janmaat provided the score-line with a look as surreal as the circumstances of the day. Newcastle United 5, Tottenham Hotspur 1 was a message to the rest of the country that loans were not just for players but entire teams. If Rafa could be convinced to stay the feeling was that United would simply be on loan to the Skybet Championship and St. James' would miss out on Premier League football than Tottenham's own White Hart Lane would when Spurs forsook it for Wembley a year later while their new White Hart Lane was constructed.

Crestfallen, Tottenham boss Pochettino admitted with regard to Rafa, "We are third in the table and Newcastle are relegated but he felt sorry for me."

Rafa himself had spent the afternoon listening to constant choruses of "Rafa Benitez, we want you to stay" coming from all parts of the ground. It would have been the easiest thing in the world for him to salute the fans, head off down the tunnel and re-emerge at whatever big name club came calling to offer the Champions League winner his next posting.

What Happened Next has long since been a key part of 'A Question of Sport' but what would happen next for Newcastle would not just be a crucial moment for the coming months but the entire future of a club if they could hold onto a man with the ambition to match that of the fans.

CHAPTER 2

THE RAFARENDUM

This was one summer 16 Rafarendum where the remainers won. Speaking after promotion was clinched against Preston in the game that was his first of the season, goalkeeper Rob Elliott reflected, "That Tottenham game, that was the start of the manager thinking, 'Well look at this place and look at what we can be'. Hopefully he is here for a long, long time and we can reach those heights again. He deserves all the credit he gets."

Newcastle have had some great managers, Sir Bobby Robson, Kevin Keegan and Joe Harvey for example. They have also had some who haven't been all they were cracked up to be, but that's too long a list and might bring back too many painful memories to mention. One thing is for sure and that is that the crowd; sometimes divided in the past over a manager's credentials, were united in being determined to do everything in their power to persuade Benitez that rather than move on to add another of Europe's major clubs to his C.V. he would be best off staying with Newcastle United, regardless of which league they were in. A front page appeal in the Evening Chronicle pleading with Benitez to stay attracted 25,000 signatures as every effort was made to persuade the man whose family home is on The Wirral to stay on Tyneside.

Despite the deep disappointment of relegation the Spurs game became a celebration not a wake. Rather than wallowing in pity that the club had gone down due to previous errors, the Toon Army heralded the fact that a leader had been found. It was a leader who everyone connected with the club had faith in, be they a player, a member of staff or a supporter.

Already in his short spell in charge, Benitez had exuded confidence and charisma. He had made a connection with people. The man from Madrid had grown up in a football mad city and had worked in similarly passionate places such as Liverpool, Milan and Naples but this was Newcastle, a place where 50,000 had come to support him and the team following relegation. Benitez had been begged to stay, to continue the job he had begun, in turning the club around.

Given all that Newcastle United represents and how much it has got wrong in the past, turning the club around is like the task facing the captains of those giant cruise ships sometimes seen in the Tyne at Shields. There can be very little room for manoeuvre but with the right person at the helm a very difficult job can be done, even if for some of the time you have to sail close to the edge.

Benitez had experienced adulation before. He'd won European trophies with Liverpool, Chelsea and Valencia and the FIFA World Club Cup with Inter, as well as the Coppa Italia with Napoli and early career promotions with two clubs in Spain. Rafa was not a man for whom success was a novelty or a flash in the pan. He is a serial winner and the crowd knew it.

Many people also knew that when Benitez replaced former England boss Steve McClaren his contract reportedly included a release clause which would allow him to walk away if Newcastle did go down.

Benitez hadn't just seen and heard the passion at Newcastle, he had felt it. "The love I could feel from the fans was a big influence in my decision" he admitted 10 days later when his decision to remain was made public. "After the last game it would have been difficult to walk away" he said, "It was amazing. I want to repay the fans."

Realising what United had to offer even to a manager of his status Rafa explained," This is a huge club and I wanted to be part of the great future I can see for Newcastle United. I'm convinced we can go up next season, stay in the Premier League for a long time and win trophies. This is a massive club and I want to stay part of it."

Shrewd operator that he is, Rafa wasn't remaining simply out of sentiment. He had been working behind the scenes to strengthen his hand. Given the outpouring of support for him on the final day, combined with the way he had got the team playing Benitez had sought assurances from the managing director Lee Charnley and owner Mike Ashley. The future direction and financing of a club about to lose the riches that come with being part of the Premier League was something that Rafa needed to steer in a positive direction.

Revealing that he didn't have to sell players and would be able to strengthen his squad, Benitez explained, "I have responsibility for football business and the most important thing is I have assurances that we will have a strong, winning, team. If I'm here it is because I am sure we can get promoted" adding, "My relationship with Lee Charnley is really good and if I ask for something he will try to help me."

Charnley was as delighted as the fans with probably the best signing he will ever make for the club, the managing director commenting, "When we brought Rafa to the club in March, we knew he was a phenomenal manager and everything we have seen from him since has only served to reinforce that. We are therefore delighted to have secured his services for the next three years and I believe with Rafa as manager it gives us the best possible chance of returning to the Premier League at the first time of asking and delivering success for this football club beyond that.

It is clear that Rafa has connected deeply with the club's supporters and we do not underestimate the role they have played in his decision to stay. He has captured the hearts and minds not just of the fans, but of everyone who has had the pleasure of working with him at the club thus far. As a world class manager we had no doubt in our minds as to the importance of retaining him at Newcastle United."

In signing a three-year contract 57 year old Benitez was committing himself to a significant spell of his career at St. James' and he wasn't hanging around for so long with the sole ambition of winning the Championship.

CHAPTER 3
SUMMER SHOPPING

The Rafalution became an easy and overused term on Tyneside, but there's no doubt it was accurate. No fewer than 33 deals were done between Benitez deciding to stay and the transfer window closing.

Astonishingly United ended up with almost as many millions in the bank as there were moves, after the ink dried on more contracts than maybe were issued in the locale when Rafa was in the locale of the Mafia in Napoli!

Benitez brought in a full team's worth of players on permanent deals as well as Christian Atsu initially on a season long loan from Chelsea. Through the 'out' door went ten players which Newcastle got top dollar for. There was no 'fire-sale' of cheap reductions as so often happens with players leaving relegated clubs. Only veteran defender Fabricio Coloccini and surplus to requirements Steven Taylor went on frees, in both cases crossing the Atlantic.

While Newcastle invested a reported £57m, an incredible amount for a Championship club, almost all of that was accounted for by the sales of just two players: Wijnaldum and Sissoko.

Knowing exactly what he wanted to equip his squad for the rigours of the Championship Rafa shipped out players he didn't want including those who might not have fancied some of the less salubrious ports of call in a tough and often less than glamourous championship campaign. Simultaneously Benitez brought in a raft of players who knew the championship. Old hands who could be called upon when the going got tough. Players such as Grant Hanley and Daryl Murphy who even if they didn't end up playing regularly would be good influences in the dressing room. These were experienced professionals who wouldn't suffer anyone getting above themselves and who could help players coming in from abroad.

In fact the trio of overseas acquisitions didn't do well, although if they stay into 2017-18 Achraf Lazaar from Palermo, Jesus Gamez from Atletico Madrid and Matz Sels from Gent will hope to do better after a season to acclimatise.

Undoubtedly though Benitez's summer shopping was successful overall as Dwight Gayle, Matt Ritchie, Ciaran Clark and Isaac Hayden to name four who cost less than Moussa Sissoko was sold for demonstrate how positive much of Rafa's wheeling and dealing was.

The first deal went through before the end of June with the last one not being completed until the last few moments of the transfer window when Sissoko's move to White Hart Lane was confirmed.

JUNE 29th - MATZ SELS

Goalkeeper

Signed from: Gent

Reported fee: £4.5m

Appearances: 9 league / 5 cup

End of term report: 4/10

Players from Belgium seemed to be gold-plated with the Premier League full of Belgian players including Chelsea and Liverpool 'keepers Thibaut Courtois and Simon Mignolet. Sels had been voted the best goalkeeper in Belgium the previous year, had Champions League experience, having helped Gent win the Belgian Pro League in 2015, and at 24 looked like a player yet to come into his best years.

Evidently signed as first choice, Sels started the season in the team but failed to impress despite keeping four clean sheets in the opening nine games. In the last of those appearances Sels' poor positioning helped gift Aston Villa a late equaliser resulting in Rafa showing his ruthless side by dropping him. Sels would not play in the Championship again, his five further outings being limited to cup-ties and with United looked ready to sell Sels come the end of the campaign.

JULY 1st - DWIGHT GAYLE, MATT RITCHIE, ANDROS TOWNSEND

The departure of Andros Townsend was felt more than any other, so much so that United made strenuous attempts to bring him back in January and it would come as no surprise if the England winger was to return to Newcastle at some point. He needed to play in the top flight though and departed to cup finalists Crystal Palace

Losing Townsend and getting Gayle and Ritchie though was a bit like losing £5 down the back of the settee and finding a tenner you'd forgotten in the back pocket of your trousers. Not only would the pair be successes individually but hitting it off together, the pair became the side's two top scorers.

JULY 1st - DWIGHT GAYLE

Striker

Signed from: Crystal Palace

Reported fee: £10.5m

Appearances: 26+6 league / 1+1 cups

Goals: 23, all league

End of term report: 9/10

Despite only signing a new contract at Selhurst Park where he had been Crystal Palace's top scorer for the past three seasons even though at times he had struggled to command a regular place in the side, Londoner Dwight Gayle jumped at the chance of signing for Newcastle.

While the same day saw Andros Townsend travel in the opposite direction for an even bigger fee, the two moves were independent of each other and United would have captured Gayle even if Townsend hadn't been destined for Selhurst Park.

Reportedly the 26 year old cost a fee of £8.5m with add-ons of a further

£1m each if he scored 20 goals in the season and Newcastle won promotion. Cheap at the price although Palace more than doubled their money having made him their record purchase when paying £4.5m to Peterborough in 2013.

Giving Gayle a five-year deal illustrated Benitez's confidence in a player who would prove himself worthy of the ultimate accolade of being handed the Newcastle number nine shirt.

Quickly off the mark with a goal on his home debut – albeit a header on the rebound from his own penalty – Dwight just kept on scoring. Opposition defences couldn't hold him as his toughest opponent proved to be his own difficulty in staying fit, a problem he will have to rectify but one which a Premier League programme of eight fewer games than in the Championship can only help.

Dwight's devastating combination of pace and technique destroyed defences of the calibre he hadn't faced since netting almost a goal every two games with The Posh in 2012-13. Then he'd come into their side in November, scored seven times in his first nine games and gone on to bag a hat trick at Blackburn. He would net two hat-tricks in his first season in the north-east, including one in the most dramatic circumstances against Norwich.

In his last season in the Premier League Dwight scored only three league goals (plus four in cups) but seems certain to do better in Newcastle colours and has already scored in the Premier League at St. James – for Palace back in 2014.

JULY 1st - ANDROS TOWNSEND

Winger

Sold to: Crystal Palace

Reported fee: £13m

Sold for the same £13m fee he had been bought for at the start of the year, due to an apparent release clause in his contract, Andros Townsend had done so well in a Newcastle shirt that he had earned a recall to the England team at the end of his half season on Tyneside.

The Londoner had got four goals in 13 games including a spectacular winner as Palace were beaten at St. James' near the end of the season. Subsequently former Toon boss Alan Pardew took The Eagles to the limit when he made Andros their record signing, beating the previous highest fee of £10m he'd paid for Yohan Cabaye.

A change of manager at Selhurst Park with one ex Toon boss replacing another as Big Sam Allardyce took over from Pards meant that Townsend was no longer playing for the man who signed him. From that springs some hope that perhaps the exciting speed-merchant may once again be on Benitez's to buy list and a player of his calibre might return to help to help Rafa re-establish The Toon in the top flight. With Dwight Gayle having revealed that "Andros Townsend said he was a great guy to play under" when the pair moved in opposite directions there's added reason to hope that the winger might yet enjoy a second spell at St. James'.

JUNE 1st - MATT RITCHIE

Winger

Signed from: Bournemouth

Reported fee: £12m

Appearances: 40+2 league / 4+2 cups

Goals: 12 league / 4 cups

End of term report: 9/10

While Andros Townsend wanted to swap the Championship for the Premier league the fact that, like Dwight Gayle, Matt Ritchie was prepared to go in the opposite direction spoke volumes for his belief in the Benitez project. It stood to reason. Ritchie was leaving a club with a ground barely one fifth the size of St. James' to come to tear up the Championship.

Ritchie had actually won the championship a year earlier with Bournemouth, scoring four more league goals in that season when the Cherries were on top than the 11 he bagged in black and white. Since picking up what would be the first of two championship medals in three seasons he'd enjoyed a terrific season in the Premier League, playing all but two games as Eddie Howe's side finished a creditable 16th and impressively won 3-1 on Tyneside.

At 26 when he signed for The Toon, Ritchie was coming into his prime as Newcastle tied him down on a five-year deal. With just under 300 league appearances under his belt when he moved to the north-east Matt had gained plenty of experience having begun his career in the Premier League with Portsmouth before a series of loans followed by a stint at Swindon where his subsequent transfer to Bournemouth caused outrage in Swindon supremo Paolo Di Canio. Two years later Ritchie's success at Bournemouth brought an international debut for Scotland, the country of Gosport born Matt 's father.

Undoubtedly Newcastle were a better team when Ritchie was playing during 2016-17. His pace, directness, ability to cross on the run, powerful shooting and dead-ball accuracy all added up to a terrific asset but over and above that he dovetailed brilliantly with his new teammates, his understanding with Jonjo Shelvey in particular making United a joy to watch.

JULY 5th - FABRICIO COLOCCINI

Central defender

Moved to: San Lorenzo

Reported fee: Free

So often Newcastle have failed to get value for money out of players but even though Fabricio Coloccini cost a reported £10m he certainly didn't short-change United for whom he played 274 times between 2008 and his final appearance at Chelsea a month before Benitez arrived.

Coloccini had been a stalwart of the Chris Hughton team who had won the Championship in 2010 when his performances earned him a place in the Championship Team of the Year.

Becoming United captain in 2011, that year he became North East Football Writers' Player of the Year with the flow of awards continuing to come his way as he was included in the PFA Team of the Year with manager Alan Pardew paying him the ultimate compliment of comparing him with the immaculate Bobby Moore.

An Argentina international, Coloccini commenced his career in Buenos Aires with Boca Juniors before the turn of the millennium and also played for San Lorenzo where he won the title in 2001. His time with San Lorenzo was as a loan player from AC Milan for whom he never played. Further loans followed with Alaves, Atletico Madrid and Villareal before a move to Deportivo La Coruna where he played over 100 games before moving to Newcastle where he would spend the best years of his career.

Coloccini's time on Tyneside was effectively up before Benitez took over but nonetheless the departure of a respected member of the old guard was a clear sign of the changing of the guard and a new regime beginning.

JULY 8th - JESUS GAMEZ

Full back

Signed from: Athletico Madrid

Reported fee: £1.5m

Appearances: 2+3 league / 2 cup

Goals: 0

End of term report: 4/10

As one former Atletico Madrid defender departed in Coloccini, another arrived in the shape of veteran full back Jesus Gamez. A former Spain

Under 23 international, Gamez had come through the ranks with Malaga where he'd spent a decade and captained the club.

Prior to making the move abroad late in his career Gamez had played for Diego Simeone at Atletico where he had used his experience when asked to perform on the other flank to his natural side.

Having been used to playing against such challenging opposition as Real Madrid and Barcelona, Gamez was eased into the English game by Benitez with a debut in the EFL Cup against Cheltenham Town before a more demanding league bow as a sub as he came on to help secure the home win over Brighton.

However he would be carried off in his first league start in the home defeat by Blackburn, play a full game in the Championship just once and appear in a meagre seven games in total as injuries combined with Paul Dummett's consistency at left back and the contest between Vurnon Anita and DeAndre Yedlin at right back contrived to make his first season outside of his home country a tough one.

JULY 9th - PAPISS CISSE

Striker

Sold to: Shandong Luneng

Reported fee: £2.5m

Papiss Cisse is unlikely to have grown up dreaming of playing for Shandong Luneng but for Newcastle, the Chinese outfit offering a sizeable fee for a 31 year old striker who had only managed to start 14 games in the previous season was certainly a dream approach, coming as it did shortly after United had invested in the purchase of Dwight Gayle.

In China, Cisse paired up with former Southampton forward Graziano Pelle and started well with five goals in his first 11 appearances but some of the memories he'd left behind at St. James will stay with the fans as much as the love of the fans would stay with the Senegal international who tweeted, 'I want to put on record my thanks and appreciation for the Newcastle fans. I will never forget them as long as I live and will be back as a supporter alongside them one day.'

JULY 11th - ISAAC HAYDEN

Midfielder

Signed from: Arsenal

Reported fee: £2.5m

Appearances: 28+5 league / 3+2 league

Goals: 2 league / 0 cup

End of term report: 8/10

Groomed though the acclaimed Arsenal youth system, 21 year old Isaac Hayden left the Emirates with Arsene Wenger's good wishes, "He's very intelligent and very good physically as well. He has good strength. I think Newcastle is a good opportunity for him.

Initially with Southend United, Hayden had been with The Gunners since he was 13 and got a couple of chances for Wenger's side in League Cup ties against West Brom and Southampton and gained Championship experience on loan to Hull who he helped to the Play-offs playing 18 times, half of them as starts.

Capped by England at Under 21 level three times during his first season with Newcastle, Hayden got off to a bright start with a goal in the victory over Reading on his third appearance and scored a beauty at Cardiff in the penultimate match.

For much of the season Rafa rotated youngster Hayden with the more experienced Jack Colback and undoubtedly as he gets older Hayden will look to prove that he is Premier League class.

JULY 21st - GRANT HANLEY

Centre half

Signed from: Blackburn Rovers

Reported fee: £5.5m

Appearances: 5+5 league / 6 cup

Goals: 1 league

End of term report: 5/10

Scotland international Grant Hanley looked to be exactly the sort of uncompromising and rugged stopper needed to deal with the physicality of the lower level Newcastle were about to find themselves in. In the previous four seasons Hanley had played over 150 times in the Championship and so was a player who could hit the ground running with no worries about his potential adaptability.

The former Rovers skipper was included in the starting line-up for the opening game disappointment at Fulham but never established himself in the side despite a goal on his second league appearance. That came over a month later as he came off the bench in the big win at QPR.

So peripheral was the Dumfries born defender that having been selected to start the opening game he didn't start another league match until February, never started consecutive Championship fixtures and began more games in the cups than the league. It would come as no surprise if he was sold during the summer as United rise in level.

JULY 22nd - GEORGINIO WIJNALDUM

Midfielder

Sold to: Liverpool

Reported fee: £25m

Having captained PSV Eindhoven to the Eredivisie title when he'd been the Dutch player of the Year, Wijnaldum had been United's marquee signing in the summer of 2015 - almost a year to the day since he'd scored against host nation Brazil in the World Cup.

At times Georginio could control a game. Easy on the eye, the Dutch master had moments of brilliance. In one match against Norwich he scored four times while one of his other top performances left an impression on Liverpool when he helped United to a convincing 2-0 win.

Just as he could be inspirational however Wijnaldum could be invisible. In particular he could go missing away from home, a point highlighted that all 11 of his goals for United came at St. James'. While it is always disappointing to lose a player of genuine talent, he didn't look likely to be up for the attritional nature of the Championship and in being sold for over £10m more than he cost it was an excellent piece of business as Benitez re-structured his squad.

AUGUST 1st - STEVEN TAYLOR

Centre-back

Moved to: Portland Timbers

Reported fee: Free

London born Steven Taylor had given long service to Newcastle, a club he called home having grown up in the area, attending Monkseaton High School. The defender played over 200 times but despite having won a medal as part of the last United squad to win the Championship in 2010 he was deemed surplus to Rafa's requirements.

A move to the USA with Portland Timbers proved to be brief as he was released by the MLS club before Christmas after which returned to the UK with joined Ipswich Town.

AUGUST 3rd - CIARAN CLARK AND MOHAMED DIAME

With the opening match of the season only 48 hours away Newcastle's squad building received a major boost with two big signings, both going on to have a positive impact on the promotion campaign although neither would play in the curtain raiser at Craven Cottage.

AUGUST 3rd - CIARAN CLARK

Centre-back

Signed from: Aston Villa

Reported fee: £5.5m

Appearances: 34 league / 2 cup

Goals: 3, all league

End of term report: 9/10

Two days after Steven Taylor followed Fabricio Coloccini out of the club, the arrival of centre back Ciaran Clark to strengthen a department that already boasted Jamaal Lascelles, Chancel Mbemba and Grant Hanley demonstrated Benitez's wish to have a strong squad and improve competition for places. Clark would emerge as the pick of the bunch, and the eventual Player of the Year.

While fans were pleased to have another new face on board, few realised how good a signing this would be. Clark had just been part of a team who had been marooned at the bottom of the league United had struggled in. Moreover he had hardly been a stalwart of that Villa side having played in fewer than half their games.

During the summer he had played twice at the European Championships for the Republic of Ireland but had scored an own goal in a draw with Sweden and lost 3-0 to Belgium. Nonetheless the tutored eye of Benitez had seen enough to believe the 26 year old would be a good addition and he was proved absolutely right.

Brought into the side after the two opening defeats Clark went on to play more games in a season than he had ever done before. The defence invariably looked more solid with him than without him with his organisational attributes adding more to the defence as a unit rather than simply what he contributed with his individual performances.

AUGUST 3rd - MOHAMED DIAME

Midfielder

Signed from: Hull City

Reported fee: £4.5m

Appearances: 25+10 league / 4 cup

Goals: 3 league / 3 cup

End of term report: 7/10

Newcastle's pulling power meant that Mohamed Diame gave up the chance of playing in the Premier League he'd just helped Hull City to reach, not least by scoring the only goal of the Play Off final to defeat Sheffield Wednesday.

The Wembley winner took the attacking midfielder into double figures in the scoring charts as he helped Hull back into the top flight. The Senegal international had been unable to prevent The Tigers from going down the year before when he'd joined them at the end of the transfer window after starting the season with West Ham where he'd been for a couple of seasons after an initial three-year spell in English football with Wigan Athletic. Prior to that Diame had played in Spain with Rayo Vallecano and Linares after beginning his career with Lens in France where he was born.

The powerful 29 year old could be a match-winner. At times his ability to clip the ball into the path of the front runners provided important goals while he chipped in with half a dozen himself including strikes at his former clubs Hull and Wigan as well as a fortunate but vital equaliser at Brighton.

AUGUST 4th - FLORIAN THAUVIN

Winger

Loaned to: Marseille

Length of loan: Full season

With eight players already brought in, one time Ligue 1 Young Player of the Year Florian Thauvin became the sixth shipped out but the first on loan.

When he arrived from Marseille for a reported £15m in August 2015 the young winger came with a massive reputation which was enhanced with three assists and a goal on his home debut. Unfortunately he flattered to deceive as that home debut was a cup game against Northampton and much of the rest of his performances could be likened to Northampton's nickname of The Cobblers.

Thauvin had quickly returned to Marseille on loan half way through the 2015-16 season but had returned to United and played for them in pre-season and scored in the opening pre-season game at Bohemian. Nonetheless it suited both player and club for him to return once again to Marseille where his season long loan was expected to become a permanent return transfer, the terms of the deal apparently ensuring this after Thauvin had turned out just three times for the club where he clearly felt at home.

Amazingly given how little Florian had impressed at Newcastle, by March reports were circulating that Barcelona were interested in him as he was called into the France senior squad for the first time. Come the end of the season Thauvin became an overwhelming winner of Marseille's Player of the Year award.

AUGUST 8th - IVAN TONEY

Forward

Loaned to: Shrewsbury Town

Length of loan: Until January 3rd 2017

20 year old Ivan Tony had made four appearances for Newcastle in the season just ended including two in the Premier League, the last at Old Trafford. Like Mohamed Diame he'd enjoyed Play-off success, having capped a long loan spell with Barnsley by appearing in the League One Play-off final for them as they defeated Millwall.

More experience was to come the former Northampton youngster's way as he was allowed to join Shrewsbury and later promotion chasing Scunthorpe. Ending the season with a decent 14 goals from his two loans, the last of them came in the Play-offs where this time it was Millwall's turn to end Ivan's hopes.

AUGUST 11th - REMY CABELLA

Midfielder

Sold to: Marseille

Reported fee: £8m

More business with Marseille where Florian Thauvin had departed for less than a week earlier. The man from Corsica had already been with Marseille for a season having initially gone there on loan as part of the deal that Thauvin transfer to Tyneside.

Having failed to find his best form in England, thankfully Cabella showed what he was capable of in 32 games on loan to Olympique de Marseille with United reputedly selling him for the same £8m fee he'd cost when bought from Montpelier with whom he had won the French title when he was a key part of the supply line to Olivier Giroud.

AUGUST 22nd - SIEM DE JONG

Midfielder

Loaned to: PSV Eindhoven

Length of loan: Full season

A class act but one who sometimes appeared to be made of glass. Injuries have haunted the career of the talented Dutch international schemer. As the captain of Ajax, De Jong had shown his quality with three goals over two legs of a Champions League encounter with Manchester City in 2012 so when he joined Newcastle in the summer of 2014 for around £6m big things were expected of a player whose brother Luuk had been on loan at Newcastle from Borussia Monchengladbach the previous season.

Siem didn't play alongside Luuk at Newcastle but did at PSV where Siem made 19 appearances, including three in the Champions League. He hit a purple patch in March with five goals (including two penalties) in three games but only played a full 90 minutes five times.

In terms of ability he could be a creative influence within Benitez's squad for the Premier League but whether he could withstand the physical rigours remains open to question.

AUGUST 23rd - KEVIN MBABU

Defender

Loaned to: Young Boys

Length of loan: Full season

Despite being sent off on his one Europa League appearance, young defender Kevin Mbabu would enjoy a productive year on loan with Young Boys in his native country of Switzerland.

Mbabu had joined United as a 17 year old in January 2013 after a solitary appearance for his first club Servette. Subsequently on loan at Rangers without playing he had played five times for Newcastle in the season Rafa Benitez took over although never for Rafa.

Playing 17 games in all competitions Mbabu helped his side to runners' up spot, one of his two goals coming in a home win over eventual champions Basel.

AUGUST 24th - DEANDRE YEDLIN, DARYL JANMAAT AND HENRI SAIVET

For the third day in a row there was squad movement with this day being particularly busy for the staff behind the scenes as right backs were traded in and out with another midfielder moving out on loan.

AUGUST 24th - DEANDRE YEDLIN

Position: Right back

Signed from: Tottenham Hotspur

Reported fee: £5m

Appearances: 21+6 league / 4+1 cup

Goals: 1, league

End of term report: 7/10

Bringing in DeAndre Yedlin meant Rafa's spending touched the £50m mark but Benitez remained in the black as the sale of Daryl Janmaat meant so far he'd raked in around £7m more.

Pacey USA international Yedlin had impressed down the road at Sunderland where he was on loan the season before when he had played at St. James' Park – his throw leading to Mitrovic's equaliser that day. During the summer he had impressed in the Copa America and now came to Newcastle at the age of 23 having had two years at Spurs where his one opportunity had lasted a meagre 12 minutes.

A permanent move to Newcastle represented a big move for a young, hungry player who Benitez knew would only improve with time and offer real competition on the right flank. Yedlin got off to a great start with his first goal in English football on his full debut at Derby and went on to total 27 appearances in the league with cup games taking that tally to over 30.

AUGUST 24th - DARYL JANMAAT

Position: Right back

Sold to: Watford

Reported fee: £7.5m

Having played in the opening two defeats, Dutch international Daryl

Janmaat followed his compatriots Georginio Wijnaldum and Siem de Jong through the exit door when he moved back into the Premier League.

Sold for 50% more than it cost to bring in the younger Yedlin, Janmaat's move was more good business by Benitez. The Dutchman had done well at Newcastle since joining from Feyenoord after the 2014 World Cup and he'd signed off with a late goal in the trouncing of Tottenham.

AUGUST 24th - HENRI SAIVET

Midfielder

Loaned to: St. Etienne

Length of loan: Full season

Each of the quartet of Premier League appearance Henri Saivet played for Newcastle had worked out at over £1m, even though none of them lasted for a full 90 minutes. The Senegal international had scored at Liverpool in the Europa League just over a month before United splashed out £5m to take him from Bordeaux.

Having not featured under Benitez it came as no surprise when ruthless Rafa released him for a year back in France. Saivet played regularly for St. Etienne, eight of his 35 appearances being in the Europa League, including two against Manchester United.

AUGUST 25th - TIM KRUL

Goalkeeper

Loaned to: Ajax

Length of loan: 31st January 2017

The Dutch exodus continued with Tim Krul's loan move to Ajax. The long-serving 'keeper had enjoyed some superb times with United for whom he had been ever-present back in 2011-12 and in total was just

15 games short of a double century. However Krul hadn't played since a 6-1 defeat at Manchester City in October since when he had sustained cruciate ligament damage playing for his country against Kazakstan.

With Cameroon international Andre Onana establishing himself as first choice at Ajax and veteran Dutchman Diederik Boer his back up, Krul's six games in Ajax colours were not for the first team but Jong Ajax, the feeder club who play in the Dutch second tier. Ajax boss Peter Bosz was not satisfied Krul was fit enough to play for the first team, where he had hoped to replace Jasper Cillessen who had moved to Barcelona.

Four days after Krul's final game for Jong Ajax in late January he was loaned again by United, this time to AZ of Alkmaar. There he played regularly but had a tough time conceding 11 goals in two legs of a Europa League tie with Lyon and shipping five at eventual champions Feyenoord and four when he went back to Ajax.

With Rafa dropping Karl Darlow for the Championship run in, Matz Sels failing to impress and Rob Elliott just coming back into the side following Darlow's demotion, Krul will hope to re-establish himself as the Toon number one and still in his twenties he's yet young for a goalkeeper. Time will tell if he gets the opportunity.

AUGUST 26th - GAEL BIGIRIMANA

Midfielder

Moved to: Coventry City

Reported fee: Free

After four years with Newcastle, 22 year old Bigirimana returned to his first club Coventry, having been back at the Sky Blues on loan the previous season.

During his first season in the north east big things were expected of Bigirimana who played in 25 games, scoring in a Premier League win over Wigan. However there had been just one more appearance for the Burundi born player who went on to play internationally for the country he had become a refugee from after playing for his adopted country of England at the FIFA Under 20 World Cup in 2013.

Despite relegation to League 2, Gael's career got back on track with Coventry for whom he played regularly in 2016-17 and had the highlight of scoring at Wembley as they beat Newcastle's FA Cup conquerors Oxford United in the final of the EFL Checkatrade Trophy.

AUGUST 28th - DARYL MURPHY AND ACHRAF LAZAAR

AUGUST 28th - DARYL MURPHY

Forward

Signed from: Ipswich Town

Reported fee: £3.5m

Appearances: 7+8 league / 2+1 cups

Goals: 5 league / 1 cup

End of term report: 7/10

Daryl Murphy had already played four games for Ipswich in the opening month of the season, the last of them the 'Old Farm' derby with Norwich.

Although he would almost always just have a single striker and already had a choice between the pace of Dwight Gayle or the power of Aleksandar Mitrovic Rafa added 33 year old Murphy for added competition and perhaps as something as an insurance policy. This was just as well given Gayle's injuries and Mitrovic's indiscipline.

Although he was yet to score in his outings for The Tractor Boys at the start of the season, Murphy had been the Championship's top scorer two seasons earlier and had hit double figures again during the year in between. Like centre back Grant Hanley from Blackburn, Murphy knew the level Newcastle would be playing at and had the nous to offer

Newcastle additional fire-power.

Murphy celebrated his move to Newcastle with his first international goal for the Republic of Ireland between his signing and his debut. It came in a World Cup qualifier away to Serbia, for whom Mitrovic had already been subbed and could only watch as his new rival for a first team place found the back of his country's net. This was an added extra for Murphy who knew he would have to fight for his place at St. James' although he'd been a shoe-in at Portman Road.

In fact Murphy would start just three more league games for United than he had already played for Ipswich but he weighed in with five championship goals, two of them off the bench. Murphy's Law saw to it that Daryl scored on his return to Mick McCarthy's side, which proved to be the first time he played a full 90 minutes in the league since his final match.

Although he didn't play a lot of games for Newcastle, the Irishman made a telling contribution, was always ready when called upon and certainly played his part ensuring he helped to get the Toon up.

AUGUST 28th - ACHRAF LAZAAR

Left back

Signed from: Palermo

Reported fee: £3m

Appearances: 0+4 league / 5 cups

Goals: 0

End of term report: 4/10

Of all the full backs in all the world, Newcastle decided to make Casablanca born Achraf Lazaar the last of their summer purchases. It might have been love at first sight for Benitez when on Valentine's Day 2015 Lazaar scored against Rafa's Napoli for Palermo.

It was Lazaar's first goal for the Sicilian club who he had joined from Varese just over a year earlier when he had gained he experience of a successful promotion by helping Palermo to promotion from Serie 'B'.

After starting over 50 Serie 'A' games in two seasons the Morocco international was brought to Newcastle for whom he was given a first taste of English football in the EFL Cup win over Wolves. Achraf would go on to start four further cup-ties but never established himself in the league line up. Never starting a Championship fixture he was restricted to four brief appearances off the bench, the longest of them giving him the final 15 minutes of a 4-0 home win over basement club Rotherham.

AUGUST 30th - ADAM ARMSTRONG

Striker

Loaned to: Barnsley

Length of loan: Full season

Appearances: 0+2 league / 0 cups. (Barnsley: 21+13 league / 1 cup)

Goals: 0. (Barnsley: 6, all league)

End of term report: 5/10

There had been considerable clamour for local lad Adam Armstrong to be given a chance as the teenager smashed 20 goals on loan to League One Coventry. Rafa listened and brought the nippy front-man off the bench in the opening two games without him being able to find the back of the net. Having gone for experience by bringing in Murphy the Gaffer elected have Armstrong continue his footballing education with another loan move, this time to Barnsley, competing at the same level as The Toon.

The Tykes would be the final visitors of the season when Adam was ineligible to play as United snatched the title from under Brighton's noses but his absence was surprising when the Newcastle squad came out for their presentation. The youngster had after all played a couple of games for the champions in addition to the 34 league appearances he made for the South Yorkshire outfit.

Having scored twice in his first three games for The Tykes the goals didn't flow as freely as they had in League One, just four more including a penalty coming the youngster's way.

Nonetheless the young Geordie remains a natural finisher as his well-taken goal for England against Argentina in the summer's FIFA Under 20 World Cup in South Korea illustrated. So far Armstrong's career has consisted of small steps and time will tell whether he can make the giant leap to playing in the Premier League for his home town team.

AUGUST 31st - CHRISTIAN ATSU, EMMANUEL RIVIERE, JAMIE STERRY, HARIS VUCKIC, SAMMY AMEOBI, KYLE CAMERON, ALEX GILLIEAD, TOM HEARDMAN AND MOUSSA SISSOKO

AUGUST 31st - CHRISTIAN ATSU

Midfielder

Signed from: Chelsea

Reported fee: On loan for the season

Appearances: 15+17 league / 1+2 cups

Goals: 5, all league

End of term report: 7/10

Newcastle United became the sixth loan of Christian Atsu's career as on the final day of the transfer window Rafa brought in his only loan signing, albeit one where United had an option to make the move permanent if the player did well enough.

Originally loaned out from Porto to fellow Portuguese club Rio Ave, the Ghanaian eventually got into the Porto side playing half a dozen Champions League games for them and helping Sir Bobby Robson's old club to retain their domestic league title for a third season running.

Always ready to snap up top young talent, Chelsea pounced, paying £3.5m for Atsu, immediately loaning him out to Vitesse Arnhem in the Netherlands for whom he played regularly before being loaned out to Everton the following season. At Everton Roberto Martinez gave him just a solitary Premier League start amongst 13 appearances for the Toffees, most of which came in the Europa League.

Another loan move to Bournemouth provided a debut in the north east in the League Cup at Hartlepool but just one more cup appearance before the player's next stop took him to Spain with Malaga where he played more, but still mainly as an impact sub.

Arriving at Newcastle as a 24 year old Christian couldn't have had an easier debut, coming off the bench in the 6-0 win at QPR. Quickly becoming an important member of the squad whether starting or coming off the bench, Atsu boosted his standing with a vital winner at Rotherham and went on to contribute four more goals including one on the night promotion was clinched against Preston and a beauty in the follow up victory at Cardiff.

Those late season strikes were well timed as Newcastle considered whether to trigger a £6.5m option to buy clause for a player who played in the last World Cup and African Cup of Nations and will hope to play in the next ones as a player who has just done well in the Premier League with Newcastle.

AUGUST 31st - EMMANUEL RIVIERE

Forward

Loaned to: Osasuna

Length of loan: Full season

At times Emmanuel Riviere can produce sublime skill which is what helped him rocket to fame with some eye-catching displays in French football with St. Etienne, Toulouse and Monaco.

Having already twice commanded sizeable fees, Riviere cost a reported

£6m when Alan Pardew decided to bring him in in the summer of 2014. His first season saw the player feature 28 times. More was expected in his second season having had a year to acclimatise but Riviere barely featured meaning his loan out came as no surprise.

Debuting in a heavily defeat at Real Madrid things got no better for club or player as a season of struggle saw Osasuna relegated with Riviere never getting his name on the score-sheet for a club who had just returned to the Primera Division.

AUGUST 31st - JAMIE STERRY

Defender

Loaned to: Coventry City

Length of loan: January 4th 2017

Appearances: 0+2 league / 1 cup. (Coventry: 16+0 league / 3 cups)

Goals: 0. (Coventry: 1 cup)

End of term report: 6/10

Young local defender Sterry was sent out to gain experience. Rafa had given him the final few minutes of the Tottenham game as Newcastle signed off for a season at the top level. Evidently seeing potential in the defender, Benitez played him for the full 120 minutes of the League Cup tie with Cheltenham before he followed Gael Bigirimana to the Sky Blues.

Regular football came Jamie's way as he turned out 20 times, even getting a first goal in the FA Cup at Morecambe. Returning in January Rafa rewarded the youngster by bringing him off the bench shortly after his return when the game was effectively already won against Rotherham. Still in Rafa's thoughts, Jamie got another brief taste of first team action at the end of the season against Cardiff and will go into 2017-18 hoping for push for first team involvement or at least follow Adam Armstrong in finding his next loan is at a higher level as he continues his football education.

AUGUST 31st - HARIS VUCKIC

Midfielder

Loaned to: Bradford City

Length of loan: January 3rd 2017

Realistically Vuckic looks to have had his chance and being out of contract in the summer of 2017 it is unlikely he would be offered a new one. No longer a player looking to unlock potential, the Slovenian will turn 25 in the first month of the 2017-18 campaign and will need something of a miracle to make it at Newcastle.

As the transfer window closed with United's promotion challenge already under way Vuckic was loaned to Bradford City. It was the latest in a long line of loans since arriving on Tyneside in 2009 as a promising teenager, one who had debuted in the Slovenian league at the tender age of 15 with Domzale.

Young enough to still play for Newcastle's Under 18s when he arrived, Vuckic was the name on everyone's lips when he scored on his debuts for both the reserves and youths. A handful of first team outings came Haris' way in his first two years at Newcastle before a month's loan with Cardiff brought a first senior goal on Valentine's Day 2012.

A highlight of his time with Newcastle came at the start of the following season when he became the hero with a Europa League winner against Greek side Atromitos. Further loans followed to Rotherham, Rangers and Wigan along with the occasional turn for The Toon. A winner for Wigan against Bradford helped persuade The Bantams to take him for the first half of the 2016-17 season but apart from goals in the EFL Checkatrade Trophy his only strike was from the penalty spot. A knee injury later restricted his chances of making a belated impression on Benitez.

AUGUST 31st - SAMMY AMEOBI

Midfielder

Loaned to: Bolton Wanderers

Length of loan: January 3rd 2017

Appearances: 0+4 all league. (Bolton: 15+5 league / 3+1 cups)

Goals: 0. (Bolton: 2 league / 2 cups)

End of term report: 3/10

The younger of the Ameobi brothers was left in no doubt about his chances under Rafa Benitez who he admitted had advised him to get a new club or go on loan. Determined to earn himself another chance at his home town club Ameobi gave his all for promotion bound Bolton in the first half of the season. This earned him another chance when his well- timed return from loan corresponded with Newcastle been short-handed in midfield after losing Diame and Atsu to the African Cup of Nations.

Unfortunately for Ameobi he couldn't feature in United's fringe squad full FA Cup sides as he had played in the competition for Bolton. However he did get two decent length run outs in the Championship followed by two brief further outings, but at the age of 25 and with Newcastle now at the top level again the chances of Sammy wearing his beloved black and white again seems remote.

AUGUST 31st - KYLE CAMERON

Defender

Loaned to: Newport County

Length of loan: 30th December 2016

Played a total of eight games for the South Wales club, six of them in League Two as they just stayed up.

AUGUST 31st - ALEX GILLIEAD

Midfielder / winger

Loaned to: Luton Town

Length of loan: 7th January 2017

Scored once in 21 games for The Hatters and added another goal in 10 loan appearances in the second half of the season for Bradford City, including one in the Play-offs.

AUGUST 31st - TOM HEARDMAN

Forward

Loaned to: Hartlepool United

Length of loan: January 3rd 2017

Made two appearances as a sub in the league and started a Checkatrade Trophy match.

AUGUST 31st - MOUSSA SISSOKO

Midfielder

Sold to: Tottenham Hotspur

Reported fee: £30m

Newcastle's summer shopping was already under way while Moussa Sissoko was increasing his value by starring for France in the European Championship finals. Seven deals had already been completed when Sissoko outshone Paul Pogba in the France midfield as the host nation contested the final of the tournament against Portugal. Sissoko was unrecognisable from the peripheral figure in so many of United's games as they'd headed out of the Premier League. Here he was unstoppable as he played with power, pace and panache. "This is a different Sissoko I've seen at Newcastle. It must be his twin brother" commented Alan Shearer with a remark echoed by many on Tyneside.

Newcastle had possessed such belief in Sissoko that they gave him a stunning six and a half year contract when buying him from Toulouse in January 2013 and when he marked his home debut with two goals in a win over Chelsea it looked like United had the Sissoko later seen in the European Championship final not the 'twin brother' Big Al reckoned he saw more often at St. James.

Sissoko missed only eight Premier League games in his three full seasons on Tyneside where at times he could be outstanding. On other occasions though Moussa could be moody and in the season just ended too often he failed to have as big an influence on games as a player of his calibre was capable of.

With ambitions to play at the glory clubs of Europe Sissoko had made it crystal clear he was not enamoured with the thought of playing in the Championship. Having spent as much as they had recouped through sales Newcastle were keen to cash in on a player who might prove to be a discontent influence in the dressing room. With the club's income massively reduced having dropped out of the Premier League with its TV riches the prospect of selling Sissoko while his stock was at its highest was important.

Everton and Spurs were keenest to take him on with Goodison Park looking like his most likely destination at one point. Certainly Toffees boss Ronald Koeman thought so with Everton having a private plane ready to whisk Sissoko to Merseyside. At the last minute though Tottenham agreed to pay the asking price Newcastle had raised in the light of the player's performances on the continent's biggest stage and with a turn quicker than a quicksilver winger, Sissoko swerved a move to Everton and signed for Spurs.

The move left Newcastle £30m to the good as what would show itself to be a terrific summer of buying and selling left Rafa ready to mount an assault on getting Newcastle back into the top flight.

Unfortunately for Tottenham it appeared that the 'twin brother' of the Euro final Sissoko arrived at White Hart Lane. Moussa would make fewer than 10 premier League starts in his first year at Spurs, fail to score and by the end of the season media reports surfaced suggesting another move.

Rafa Benitez's summer signings meant United were now able to field an XI entirely made up of Rafa recruits along with a sub:

SELS

YEDLIN/GAMEZ   **HANLEY**   **CLARK**   **LAZAAR**

HAYDEN   **DIAME**

RITCHIE   **ATSU**   **MURPHY**

GAYLE

Pitting Rafa's recruits against Rafa's releases would make for a fascinating match especially with some of the released players being high quality and departing to remain at the top level. Having sold nine players in the summer the Select XI below includes two of the eleven players loaned out during the summer transfer window, namely Tim Krul and Siem De Jong.

KRUL

JANMAAT   **COLOCCINI**   **TAYLOR**   **BIGIRIMANA**

TOWNSEND   **WIJNALDUM**   **DE JONG**   **SISSOKO**

CISSE   **CABELLA**

Rafa had completely re-structured his squad. Moving players on can be harder than persuading players to sign but Benitez succeeded in trimming his squad, making around £30m profit and yet ending up with a squad where there was competition all over the pitch, an injection of Championship know-how and the re-invigoration of some young, hungry players. As the transfer window closed with Newcastle's slow start already beginning to become just a memory the Toon army could look forward to a season where the team would be United at last.

CHAPTER 4
PRE-SEASON

Newcastle's pre-season was low key and focussed. With the season starting at Fulham on fifth August, United swung into action just three weeks earlier with a gentle run out in Dublin against Bohemian. Four days later there was a short hop for the Toon Army to Doncaster's Keepmoat Stadium. This was followed by a match in Belgium and in turn a visit to Phil Brown's Southend United. Finally as the build-up continued with a game every few days Vitesse Arnhem were welcomed to St. James'. Games every few days of course was something the players and fans were going to have to get used to as a league campaign of 46 fixtures stretched ahead. With cup competitions but hopefully not Play-offs to contend with the season could easily consist of over 50 matches but as the warm up games got under way Rafa was in the process of recruiting a squad deep enough to cope.

A week's training in County Kildare in Ireland culminated in a run out for 22 players and goals for six at Dalymount Park. Matt Ritchie got the first goal of 2016-17 and Dwight Gayle also got his first for the club, while the soon to depart Thauvin (on loan) and Wijnaldum also got on the score-sheet along with Mitrovic with a penalty and young Aarons. In addition to Ritchie and Gayle, Matz Sels, Jesus Gamez and Isaac Hayden all enjoyed their first appearances for their new club.

Enjoying first appearances in the sun at Dalymount Park was one thing, at Doncaster there was work to be done. Looking sluggish United found themselves two down at the interval against a home side who were about to embark on a successful promotion campaign of their own. A first United goal from Hayden early in the second half and a late equalizer from Perez at least ensured a draw against the League Two side from what was a competitive work-out for this early in pre-season.

If Doncaster was competitive then the weekend trip to Belgium to face Lokeren contained the unusual sight of two red cards in a pre-season game. Two minutes from time Jesus Gamez and the home team's Marco

Miric were sent off after a bout of pushing out of keeping with a slow paced game, where a brace from Perez and one each from Janmaat and Shelvey had a 4-0 victory wrapped up with over 40 minutes still to play.

While the 48th minute marked the end of the scoring at Lokeren, the same minute saw the first goal at Southend three days after the brief visit to Belgium. Anita took the honours here with a spectacular shot before Gouffran added another late on, while Grant Hanley got a comfortable first run out since his move from Blackburn.

Pre-season still seemed to be in its early stages after four typically slow-paced games, notwithstanding the red cards in Lokeren and the little bit of edge at Doncaster. Suddenly though it was dress rehearsal time as United welcomed Dutch outfit Vitesse Arnhem to St. James' just six days before the curtain was due to come up at Fulham, where Newcastle needed to get off to a good start.

Playing at home in their new blue and orange away strip seemed incongruous but it didn't seem to do any harm as United sailed into a 3-0 lead with Ritchie and Gayle introducing themselves to home fans by getting on the score-sheet – as did Jack Colback with a rare header.

There were worries about the heart of the defence consisting of Lascelles and Hanley though as twice goals were conceded from set-pieces and co-incidentally or not Hanley was subbed a minute after the second of them just past the hour mark.

Nonetheless the side who lined up for the real kick-off to the season at Fulham was the same XI that began the final friendly. The 3-2 win against Vitesse meant Newcastle would go to Craven Cottage unbeaten in 11 games and ready to start the season as they meant to go on. Some supreme optimists even called talk-in show 'Total Sport' on BBC Newcastle to speculate that United would go the whole season unbeaten.

This though ignored the fact that The Championship is a tough league where the sheer volume of games, commitment of workmanlike teams and the vagaries of the refereeing can mean that things don't always go to plan. The key was to make sure that despite the set-backs that would inevitably arrive along the way, Newcastle stuck to Rafa's plan. Benitez clearly had the road back to the Premier League mapped out and while there would be the odd diversion to negotiate, the signs were pointing in the right direction. With the transfer window still open even after the first 15 points had been played for, clearly while the players' pre-season work was done, Rafa still had plenty to do to prepare for the journey.

CHAPTER 5
FALSE START

With the scene set, the Toon Army travelled to London ready to start the promotion party with a win and a weekend to celebrate in the capital. The transfer window was still open but the squad had already been overhauled and looked custom made to storm the championship...

FULHAM 1   NEWCASTLE UNITED 0

Craven Cottage

Friday 5th August 2016

SCORERS:

Smith   45   0-1 (Newcastle score always first)

On the morning the Football League kicked off for the vast majority of clubs, hot favourites Newcastle were already propping up the embryonic table. This was a result of having lost the season curtain raiser on the Friday night before the watching Sky cameras and a crowd of almost 24,000 – almost a third of whom had travelled from Tyneside to see the big kick-off.

If Newcastle needed a warning sign of what could befall the club if instant promotion wasn't achieved, Craven Cottage was an ideal place to find out. Having been in the Premier League for twice as many years than the Magpies managed since their most recent dip into the Championship, The Cottagers were about to start their third season outside the big league. They had found it tough going having finished 17th and 20th rather than challenging for promotion.

Moreover with parachute payments drying up the London club had sold their main asset the day before the match – Ross McCormack going to newly demoted Aston Villa with Fulham unable to hang on to a man who had bagged 42 goals in two years for a struggling side.

Led onto the pitch in their new blue and orange kit by new skipper Jamaal Lascelles and with half the outfield players making their (competitive) debuts United looked almost unrecognisable from the previous season, but by the end of the evening looked only too like the side who had gone down. Bereft of cohesion Newcastle could have few complaints about taking nothing from the game – bar a grumble over the non-award of what should have been a penalty after Ryan Tunnicliffe didn't so much handle the ball as autograph it.

That controversy though couldn't mask the fact that despite the new arrivals at St. James, the unbeaten pre-season and the Rafa fuelled optimism, beneath it all Newcastle would need to be a lot better than this. "It's a wake-up call. We will have games more difficult than this one" observed the Gaffer, while in the TV studio ex Gaffer Steve McClaren allowed himself to consider that bringing success to Newcastle might be harder than first thought.

Matz Sels, Grant Hanley, Isaac Hayden, Matt Ritchie and Dwight Gayle all debuted with moderate success, Ritchie looking better when moving from the left to right after half time. The only goal of the game had arrived moments before the teams made their way to the dressing rooms in the quaint cottage in the corner of the ground. Having scored only twice in 21 outings in the previous campaign Matt Smith headed what proved to be the winner for former Watford boss Slavisa Jokanovic, who no doubt would have been pleased his fellow Serb Aleksandar Mitrovic was suspended.

UNITED: Sels, Janmaat, Lascelles, Hanley, Dummett, Anita, Hayden (Shelvey 77), Colback (Aarons 61), Ritchie, Perez (Armstrong 70), Gayle.

Unused: Darlow, Mbemba, Gamez, Sterry.

Attendance: 23,922

Referee: Simon Hooper

NEWCASTLE UNITED 1   HUDDERSFIELD TOWN 2

Saturday 13th August 2016

SCORERS:

Wells	45+1	0-1
Gayle	**60**	**1-1**
Payne	82	1-2

As 52,000 made their way to St. James' that opening night defeat at Fulham was thought to be surely just a blip – something to produce the wake-up call Rafa had referred to. Huddersfield would surely not be strong enough to threaten, especially with memories of a 5-1 hiding handed out to Spurs on the last day of the previous season as United defiantly signed off their top-flight tenure with a 'see you soon' message.

A spectacular pre-match display organised by Gallowgate flags must have made The Terriers think they'd been entered into Crufts, so high class were their surroundings. While Newcastle had won their last home game 5-1, the West Yorkshire outfit had lost at home by the same score-line on the final day of the previous season, meaning they'd conceded nine goals in their last two games of the campaign in which they'd finished 19th. Huddersfield had never finished higher than 16th in their four years since promotion and having not won on Tyneside since the days of Jackie Milburn, not many people fancied the chances of a team bundled out of the League Cup at Shrewsbury in mid-week before 50,000 fewer people than were ready to roar Rafa's boys on.

Mo Diame was handed his debut playing behind striker Gayle who along with Sels, Hayden and sub Ritchie was making his home debut but there was no place in the squad for Moussa Sissoko who had been speculating on the dream of a move to Real Madrid. Clearly the prospect of playing Huddersfield left the France international less than enthralled.

Once the match got going the paying public had their fears about a lower level of football confirmed. The place was slow, the quality poor and Newcastle looked sluggish and dis-jointed. New Town boss David Wagner had taken his new look squad on a pre-season survival trip to

Sweden where their bonding mission had seen them cope for themselves with only basic equipment. If that helped them develop a siege mentality all they were missing at St. James' was the siege as the home side failed to match the co-ordination the fans had demonstrated in the flag display.

Just as people were preparing to for a half-time pint or brew the break-through came – but at the wrong end when former Bradford hit-man Nakhi Wells sent Newcastle in having just conceded for the second game in a row.

Determined to show the fans they had what it takes, United came out with renewed vigour and got their first goal of the campaign on the hour mark when Gayle got off the mark. Gayle scored from the rebound after Danny Ward denied him from the penalty spot, following Mark Hudson's handball.

As relief flooded around St. James' a winner was hoped for but when it arrived, astonishingly it went to the visitors. Eight minutes from time 'keeper Matz Sels hesitated allowing Jack Payne to score his first goal since a move from Southend United.

Unable to engineer an equaliser, even after sacrificing full back Daryl Janmaat for forward Adam Armstrong, Newcastle ended the day pointless after two games leaving Rafa to admit, "We weren't expecting this kind of performance" as The Lads lost at home for the first time since his appointment. While Huddersfield found themselves joint top, probably only their most ardent supporters expected them to last the pace but to their credit they would be serious contenders all season. Thankfully so would Newcastle but after this false start realisation set in that any rewards would have to be worked hard for and Rafa still had plenty to do to get his squad in shape.

UNITED: Sels, Janmaat (Armstrong 83), Mbemba, Lascelles, Dummett, Anita, Hayden Shelvey, Aarons (Ritchie 45), Diame (Perez 75) Gayle.

Unused: Darlow, Clark, Colback, Gamez

Attendance: 52,079

Referee: Oliver Langford

CHAPTER 6

'SIXY' FOOTBALL

Having given the rest of the league a head start Rafa's revival took off in scintillating style with six wins in a row, culminating in a record equalling 6-0 victory at QPR which jettisoned United into the automatic promotion places.

Despite the opening defeats the 48,209 who turned up on a Wednesday night for the visit of Jaap Stam's Reading were undimmed in their belief that Rafa would be as capable of finding success in the Championship as he had been in the Champions League. Although they would prove to be promotion challengers throughout the campaign the Royals were no match for Newcastle who waltzed to a 4-1 win to put the first points of the season on the board. These were speedily added to with a first away win of the calendar year at Bristol City three days later.

Basement division Cheltenham were comfortably dismissed in the opening cup-tie of the season at St. James' before Brighton rocked up on Tyneside. Under Chris Hughton, The Seagulls would be The Magpies main rivals as the season wore on, but their unbeaten record ended as the first international break of the season arrived with Benitez's boys up to seventh.

Former United caretaker manager Nigel Pearson had left his old side Leicester on the brink of a fairy-tale but could only wonder at promotion bound Newcastle as United's winning sequence resumed with a 2-0 win at the Ipro Stadium, but if Pearson was impressed with Newcastle climbing into the Play Off places for the first time that was nothing to the bemusement Jimmy Floyd Hasselbaink felt when his QPR outfit were demolished 6-0 on their own patch as Rafa's men moved into an automatic spot.

Hasselbaink hails from Suriname in South America as does Ruud Gullitt, but while Gullitt's wish for sexy football was only glimpsed in his time at Newcastle his fellow Dutch international saw for himself the sixy football Newcastle were now producing: six successive wins finishing with a 6-0 score-line showed United were into their stride - with an even better run to follow starting later in the same month!

NEWCASTLE UNITED 4   READING 1

St. James'

Wednesday 17th August 2016

SCORERS:

Hayden	**20**	**1-0**
McCleary	45p	1-1
Ritchie	**50p**	**2-1**
Gayle	**69**	**3-1**
Gayle	**89**	**4-1**

Ciaran Clark made his debut but this was a night focussed on Newcastle's attacking prowess as United scored four times and could have had more. Dwight Gayle bagged two and had another ruled out for offside while Matt Ritchie converted a penalty after Isaac Hayden had opened the scoring.

Ex-Arsenal man Hayden's first goal in black and white came with a well-placed shot after he was fed by Yoan Gouffran 20 minutes into the game to settle any home nerves, but encouraged by United's hesitant start to the season Reading worked their way back into the match and went in at the interval level as United conceded on the stroke of half time as they had done in both of their previous matches. The equaliser came via the first of the game's two penalties when debutant Clark sent John Swift sprawling. Eight minutes earlier Roy Beerens had hit the bar so when Garath McCleary scored from the spot the visitors felt worthy of a share of the spoils.

That feeling wasn't to last long though as five minutes after the re-start it was the home team's turn to have a penalty, Gouffran being fouled by former Cardiff defender Chris Gunter leaving Matt Ritchie to give Ali Al-Habsi no chance from the spot.

With Yann Kermorgant prominent in most of their best moves Reading tried to work their way back into the game before Gayle provided United with some breathing space when he made it 3-1 with little over 20 minutes to go. Young Hayden had stung Al-Habsi's palms but the 'keeper could only admire Gayle's goal which took the match out of Reading's reach. The striker seemed too far out when he took aim with a dead-ball from 30 yards out at the Gallowgate End but as the free-kick whistled into the top corner Newcastle were on their way. When the influential Hayden set Gayle up with a minute to go the man from Palace further deflated The Royals with his second of what had been a first step on the road back to the Premier League.

Stam sought to assert that regardless of the heavy defeat his team had been the better side, saying, "I think if you look at the game in total we were the better team in how we played" but Benitez was prophetic in his summary, when after reflecting on the fact that this result stopped the bad start in its tracks he showed he was already well aware of what it would take to get out of a tough league over 46 fixtures, "Today we showed character" he said, "a good reaction after the goal we conceded and that's what we have to do: play well sometimes and show character all the time."

In the months ahead Newcastle wouldn't always play well but they consistently managed to dig out results. Sometimes there would be slick and spectacular shows but consistency is the name of the game when it comes to winning promotion and The Magpies would relentlessly maintain that consistency, putting enough distance between them and the chasing pack that when the points per game ratio slowed up towards the end of the season, only Brighton could seriously threaten them.

UNITED: Sels, Anita, Mbemba, Clark, Dummett, Hayden, Shelvey, Ritchie (Aarons 90), Perez (Lascelles 76), Gouffran (Colback 84), Gayle.

Unused: Darlow, Hanley, Janmaat, Armstrong.

Attendance: 48,209

Referee: Andy Madley

Post-match league position: 22nd

BRISTOL CITY 0 NEWCASTLE UNITED 1

Ashton Gate

Saturday 20th August 2016

SCORER:

Gayle	**19**	**1-0**

Having won their first three games of the season for the first time since 2001-02 and with the Toon in town, Bristol City attracted their first 20,000+ gate in two decades and their biggest since an FA Cup clash with Chelsea in January 1990. Two years of redevelopment at Ashton Gate led to the upper tier of the Lansdown Road Stand being open to Robins fans for the first time, but safety requirements prevented the attendance threatening that Chelsea gate of just over 2,000 more.

Those who did squeeze in – including a vociferous sold out 2,501 from Tyneside – saw a game of few chances but the travelling support had one golden moment when Dwight Gayle sent them into raptures, scoring the game's only goal right in front of them early on when he sublimely controlled a terrific ball from Mo Diame leaving City boss Lee Johnson to admit, "We lost to one quality finish after being out by a great ball."

He wouldn't be the last opposition manager to be undone by United's quality as the season wore on. For Newcastle the victory was a first on the road of the calendar year but happy trips home would become a regular occurrence.

On a blustery day in the south-west this game set the tone for much of the season. Against determined opposition United had to earn the right to play by matching City's endeavour and allowing quality to tell when the opportunity arrived. For Rafa the Championship undoubtedly was not the standard he was used to but as one of the world's top bosses he knew how to deal with what was required and noted, "It's great to have a team who can go forward and score goals but you also need organisation and team spirit to get results." On an afternoon when Lee

Johnson's side had played ugly with balls pumped into the box on a tricky afternoon weather wise, United had stood firm, produced their first clean sheet of the season and moved on to the next match with all three points in the bank.

UNITED: Sels, Anita, Mbemba, Lascelles, Clark, Ritchie, Hayden (Shelvey 87), Colback, Gouffran, Diame (Perez 63), Gayle (Aarons 88).

Unused: Darlow, Dummett, Hanley, Sterry.

Attendance: 22,513

Referee: Tony Harrington

Post-match league position: 17th

NEWCASTLE UNITED 2 CHELTENHAM TOWN 0

St. James'

Tuesday 23rd August 2016, EFL Cup 2nd round.

SCORER:

Perez	45+2	1-0
Perez	47	2-0

Rafa's rotation was already becoming a talking point. Regular changes would become the norm with those wanting a settled side having their arguments undermined as Benitez's approach produced the results. You can criticise a losing manager but if you're winning who is to say you should be doing something different, particularly if you've made success a byword throughout your career? Benitez had taken a long hard look at what the Championship involved and clearly was ready to rotate in order to keep players fresh for the long haul ahead with 46 league fixtures to fulfil. Play offs were not on the agenda. However cup ties were and the visit of Cheltenham brought Aleksandar Mitrovic to the races.

Mitro's inclusion and whether Newcastle should play with two up top, partnering Mitrovic with Gayle was as much the talk of pubs and clubs as whether Rafa should pick his best XI and stick with it or utilise his squad to manage the demands of the fixture list.

If those lengthy debates were carried out over a half time pint then those participating in the debate might have missed both of the evening's goals as Ayoze Perez scored deep into first half injury time and then almost immediately after the re-start.

Rotation was expected by everyone on this occasion of course as The League Cup brought Cheltenham Town to Tyneside for the first time. The League Two side had lost just one of their opening five fixtures but couldn't name a full allocation of substitutes even for their most high profile game of the season. Thankfully United had plenty of subs and they needed them as injuries befell the side. Six of those named on the bench the previous weekend at Bristol – including Perez - were unsurprisingly drafted into the starting line-up which brought eight changes including a debut for 31 year old Jesus Gamez, a first start for Jamie Sterry and a first appearance of the season for Mitrovic.

However Newcastle had to make two enforced substitutions during the first half with the game goalless, and soon even a sub had to be subbed with match-winner Perez in the wars too and scoring while heavily bandaged – and he wasn't the only one as Dwight Gayle also had to play with some unexpected headwear. Having come on for the concussed Mitrovic, Gayle had to be replaced himself by Anita. While he hadn't scored in his 21 minutes on the pitch Dwight had left his mark with the assist for Perez's second goal.

To the frustration of Cheltenham boss Gary Johnson - father of the Bristol City boss faced a few days earlier - Gayle wasn't picked up when he came back on after treatment to curl home a spectacular opener. Having doubled the lead within a couple of minute of actual playing time Perez had chances to celebrate his first brace for the club by getting another and taking the match ball home but 2-0 was comfortable enough to ensure progression to the next round which would bring a home tie with Wolves.

Other than the injuries, particularly a worrying one that would de-rail speed merchant Rolando Aaarons for the season, Rafa the Gaffer went home happy enough with the night's work, noting, "When you change the team and win, the squad is stronger."

UNITED: Darlow, Sterry, Lascelles, Hanley, Gamez, Aarons (Gouffran 24), Shelvey, Colback, Perez, Diame, Mitrovic (Gayle 38 / Anita 59).

Unused: Sels, Dummett, Hayden, Mbemba

Attendance: 21,972

Referee: Steve Martin

NEWCASTLE UNITED 2   BRIGHTON & HOVE ALBION 0

Wednesday 27th August 2016

SCORERS:

| Lascelles | 15 | 1-0 |
| Shelvey | 63 | 2-0 |

A 2-0 mid-week win over Cheltenham may have been routine but the same score-line against The Seagulls was a distinctly bigger prize than beating the pair of Robins defeated during the previous week, although perhaps Brighton's red shirts made them look as easy prey as the previous opponents.

Chris Hughton however returned to St. James' having led his club to an unbeaten start that brought them into the match as table toppers. So far they'd been impregnable on the south coast boasting a 100% record with 10 goals scored and none conceded from three games. On the road they'd taken creditable draws from Derby and Reading as well as graduating from a mid-week cup-tie at Oxford with a 4-2 win. Newcastle United though would prove to be a tougher proposition with the Toon army being bigger than the combined attendances of their three previous away games combined and with a Gallowgate flag display and an aerial fly-past carrying a banner wishing good luck to Rafa and NUFC Newcastle evidently had at least one friend on high.

Both goals came from set pieces. Fifteen minutes in Matt Ritchie curled in an inviting left footed ball which skipper Jamaal Lascelles latched onto, to head home from fully 15 yards having completely lost his marker and got a free run at the ball to allow him to get plenty of power into his header. Later Jonjo Shelvey's free kick had plenty of pace on the ball but it was placement not power which beat David Stockdale in the Albion goal. Shelvey had sized up the four-man wall and brilliantly bent his shot around them, the ball curling back from just outside the post to creep just inside it in what was a superb example of top class technique.

Both goals were right out of the top drawer but they would have been bettered if not for the crossbar. Yoan Gouffran's status at the club had been indicated by his new squad number of 20 compared to the 11 he'd worn previously. Disappointing in the Premier League, and having turned 30 since the end of the previous season, Gouffran wasn't expected to be an influential player in the promotion campaign but had started the season well and was so unfortunate not to mark his 100th appearance for the club with a goal when he cut in from the left, worked his way into a shooting position and leathered a shot from way outside the box that cannoned back off the bar. Re-invigorated under Rafa, Gouffran's transformation was proving to be a microcosm of Benitez's talent for maximising the resources at his disposal.

Crucially the manager getting the best out of his players wasn't just being done on an individual basis but collectively as well. United were living up to their name, working for each other and without anyone getting carried away – least of all the manager - it seemed clear that having taken nine points out of nine the disappointing start was already a thing of the past. Newcastle, now one place outside the play off places after this victory, were so clearly heading in one direction that they might sign Harry Styles before the transfer window closed in the coming few days.

Like the person who keeps buying raffle tickets until they get a winner, having finally got his first goal for the club after over 30 shots Jonjo Shelvey spoke about the campaign which even after five games still had over 40 fixtures to go, saying of Newcastle's place in the championship, "The club shouldn't be there, so it's time for us now to get us back out of it."

In the final analysis of course both Newcastle and Brighton would get out of the championship but there was a long, long way to go as the last game of the first month of the season was completed with work still to be done by Rafa as the last days of the transfer window ticked down and several of his squad disappeared on the first international break of the campaign.

UNITED: Sels, Anita (Gamez 72), Mbemba, Lascelles, Dummett, Ritchie, Hayden, Shelvey, Gouffran (Yedlin 88), Diame (Colback 81), Perez.

Unused: Darlow, Clark, Hanley, Armstrong.

Attendance: 49,196

Referee: Keith Stroud

Post-match league position: 4th

SLAMMING SHUT

As the international break gave time to pause and take stock of the start to the season the opening defeats had been firmly put behind The Lads, whose more recent results restored all of the pre-season optimism. Undoubtedly The Magpies seemed to have the strongest squad in the division but in terms of quality and quantity but Benitez hadn't stayed in order to take chances with ifs, buts and maybes.

Understanding the strain that a long hard season would take; a season where in every game the opposition would see you as the league's biggest scalp and raise their game, Rafa was determined to further strengthen his squad as an insurance policy against things that could so easily go wrong. He had seen players fall like nine-pins in the cup game with Cheltenham and like all insurance policies you hope you don't have to rely upon them but you feel safer knowing they're there.

So it was that in the closing days of the transfer window, while there wasn't a game on the horizon for a week or two Rafa the Gaffer was working hard behind the scenes to ensure that he would bring success to the north east.

Benitez added three more new faces. Ghana international midfielder Christian Atsu arrived on loan for a season from Chelsea. Previously with Porto and having experienced loans with Rio Ave, Vitesse Arnhem, Everton, Bournemouth and Malaga, Atsu would mark his first start with a winning goal and also be on the mark on the night promotion was mathematically ensured as he featured in over 30 league games, just over half of them from the bench.

Several signings had been players steeped in championship experience as Benitez brought in people not just with experience but relevant experience. Former Sunderland forward Daryl Murphy fitted that bill after half a dozen seasons with Ipswich Town with whom he had been the championship's top scorer in 2014-15. The Republic of Ireland cap had already played in four games of the new season for The Tractor Boys, signing off with an appearance in the 'Old Farm' derby against Norwich. He celebrated his move to Newcastle with a goal for the Republic four minutes after coming off the bench against Serbia – for whom Aleksandar Mitrovic had already been subbed.

Least surprising of the latest newcomers was Palermo left back Achraf Lazaar, not least because the Morocco international had been spotted in the stands at United's game with Brighton. Benitez had seen Lazaar at close quarters previously, not least when he had scored for Palermo against Rafa's Napoli on Valentine's Day the previous year.

St. James' Park and the training ground are top facilities but there's only so much room so the out-door was in full use too with outward loans for: Emmanual Riviere (Osasuna), Adam Armstrong (Barnsley), Jamie Sterry (Coventry City), Sammy Ameobi (Bolton), Haris Vuckic (Bradford City), Kyle Cameron (Newport County), Alex Gilliead (Luton Town), Tom Heardman (Hartlepool United) and the big one. As the clock ticked past 11.00 p.m. on the night the window closed Moussa Sissoko was sold to Spurs for a handsome fee, reported to be £30m.

Sissoko had starred at the European Championships during the summer but hadn't been as impressive on a consistent basis for Newcastle so selling him for big money made sense as Newcastle needed players ready and able to perform week in week out regardless of the sometimes less than glamourous grounds of the Championship. Spurs were to enjoy a stellar season but Sissoko's struggle to reach double figures in terms of Premier League starts for Mauricio Pochettino's talented side further illustrated that this was yet another example of Benitez getting things right off the pitch as well as on it.

DERBY COUNTY 0 NEWCASTLE UNITED 2

Ipro Stadium

Saturday 10th September 2016

SCORERS:

Gouffran	20	**1-0**
Yedlin	90+1	**2-0**

It wasn't just Newcastle who had been busy in the last days of the transfer window, The Rams had raided the piggy bank and in response to only scoring a single league goal all season had three forward players making their debuts. Matej Vydra, Ikechi Anya and James Wilson were the main attractions for the home fans in a crowd of just over 30,000 at what remained The Ipro Stadium until it reverted to the name of Pride Park two and a half months after United's visit.

Nigel Pearson's Rams had lost to local rivals Burton Albion in their last game before the international break so there had been much to agonise over at the club and a visit from Rafa's rampant side was probably the last thing everyone except their bank manager wanted. Of United's newcomers only Lazaar got on the bench, if not the pitch as Benitez took his time to blend them into the squad.

United went ahead in the 20th minute, one minute later than they'd taken the lead in the previous away match at Bristol. Fresh from scoring last time out, Shelvey would claim both assists and was quickly becoming Newcastle's most influential player, so much of United's creativity emanating from his radar and ability to execute the range of passes in his locker. It was from Jonjo's corner that the in-form Gouffran volleyed home an equaliser almost as spectacular as his effort would have been had it gone in rather than smacking the bar against Brighton.

While the most recent signings had to be patient, Deandre Yedlin wasted no time in making his mark. The USA international who had played at Newcastle the previous season for Sunderland (when his foul throw led to Mitrovic's equaliser) had come off the bench for the final few minutes of the Brighton game and had since crossed the Atlantic to play for the USA in a World Cup qualifier against St. Vincent. DeAndre had been part of a 6-0 away win for the States and would soon feature in another 6-0 away win for United but for now he had a key role to play in this match.

Already in added time, Newcastle's first instinct was to retain possession and secure the victory but Shelvey took the opportunity to find Perez from a flag kick with Yedlin getting the final important touch.

That second goal helped Newcastle into an automatic promotion spot for the first time. Level on points with third placed Barnsley United's goal difference of plus six after as many games was the best in the division. The Tykes were on plus five, (having scored more than Newcastle) as were leaders Huddersfield four points ahead of United. Birmingham City, Norwich City and Fulham occupied the remaining Play-off berths level on 11 points with four sides a further point behind while Brighton had slipped into the bottom half of the table.

Two of Pearson's new forwards were subbed as Derby once again drew a blank and the newcomers would get scant chance to impress to make plans with Nigel as Pearson left under a month later, apparently after a disagreement with the club owner Mel Morris who wanted to use drones to observe the former Newcastle caretaker manager's training sessions.

Tactically Rafa didn't need drones, just his attention to detail during preparation. In a disciplined team performance Derby's attacking threats were constantly negated, not least through forward thinking players such as Gouffran and Ritchie working their socks off, finding that assisting their full backs was as valuable to the team as providing assists going forward. Gouffran's volley in this match was the latest in a serious of picture goals the Magpies had produced during this thrilling run but almost unnoticed the defence had now ticked past 400 minutes since they had conceded.

No-one would notice the defence in the next match either. Who would when the attack score six away from home but there are two main elements to a football team and Newcastle were hitting the magic combination of getting both defence and attack right at the same time. "The main thing for me has been to see the team working as a team from the strikers to the 'keeper" noted Rafa, who you felt was looking more and more like a villain with a masterplan from a Bond film – except that Rafa was the good guy and given the sixy football maybe more 006 than 007.

UNITED: Sels, Anita, Mbemba, Lascelles, Dummett, Ritchie, Shelvey, Colback, Gouffran (Yedlin 73), Diame (Hayden 88), Gayle (Perez 76).

Unused: Darlow, Clark, Lazaar, Mitrovic

Attendance: 30,405

Referee: James Linington

Post-match league position: 2nd

QUEENS PARK RANGERS 0 NEWCASTLE UNITED 6

Loftus Road

Tuesday 13th September 2016

SCORERS:

Shelvey	12	1-0
Perez	30	2-0
Shelvey	48	3-0

Clark	56	4-0
Mitrovic	63	5-0
Hanley	79	6-0

Newcastle's promotion charge had been building. Consistent wins had seen a rapid climb into the top two. Decent teams had been beaten with the defence tight and some truly spectacular goals providing plenty of excitement, but this mid-week trip to the capital made a statement to the rest of the football world.

A six goal winning margin away from home equalled a club record on a night when Rafa's rotation saw the sixy football climax with such a sensational score-line even though Benitez kept his ultimate weapon Dwight Gayle on the bench! "It's hard to take, but I must say that Newcastle are a great team with big players and you could see that" observed Hoops boss Hasselbaink but Benitez still wasn't satisfied, "We can still improve" he insisted.

It was a far cry from the opening game of the season just two miles away, 39 days earlier at Craven Cottage when United couldn't score. Here The Magpies were scoring for fun: Ayoze Perez had already had the ball in the back of the net without it counting before Jonjo Shelvey opened the scoring with just 12 minutes on the clock, his shot clipping off former Wolves captain Karl Henry but his misfortune was nothing compared to former United man James Perch who sadly left the field on a stretcher six minutes later. He would be missing for a month but would make a full recovery and would play the full game at St. James' later in the season.

It took United just another dozen minutes after the delay for Perch's injury to extend the lead Perez netting but a two goal interval lead was modest reward for a dominant performance, the home side having just a solitary first half effort to remind Matz Sels there was a game going on at the other end.

Those behind the Belgian 'keeper's goal would see some action when the teams changed ends. Indeed it took just three minutes of the second half to extend he lead and extinguish any hopes Hasslebaink's side had of coming back into the match. This wasn't the Rangers side of '84 who infamously fought back from being 0-4 down to United at the break to draw 5-5 on their plastic pitch. It wasn't just the fact that Shelvey scored again that deflated the home side, it was also the quality of the strike that made onlookers realise the visitors were a class apart.

Ciaran Clark got his first goal since his summer move with a header from Matt Ritchie's 56th minute corner and seven minutes later it was 5-0 as Mitrovic got on the end of a ball in from debutant Christian Atsu before Grant Hanley joined Clark in claiming his first United goal to complete the scoring with 11 minutes to go.

It wasn't the greatest night for Rangers' goalkeeper Alex Smithies whose former club Huddersfield lost to a late goal at Brighton leaving the Rafalution just a single point behind the pace-setting Terriers, albeit just in the automatic places courtesy of being the only team in the championship with a better goal–difference than third placed Barnsley who had enjoyed a handsome 4-0 away win of their own that night at Wolves where all the goals came in the final 17 minutes.

The Tykes would be in the bottom half of the table before they won again though as they fell away as so many of United's challengers would. Of the sides who had come down with Newcastle Norwich were fourth but would fall away while Aston Villa had slumped to 18th. This though was a night for Tyneside to savour, one of the highlights of a season to remember as Benitez ensured Newcastle bounced straight back.

UNITED: Sels, Anita, Lascelles, Clark, Dummett (Hanley 65), Gouffran (Atsu 61), Hayden, Shelvey, Ritchie, Perez, Mitrovic (Yedlin 74).

Unused: Darlow, Colback, Diame Gayle

Attendance: 17,404

Referee: Andy Davies

Post-match league position: 2nd

RECORD AWAY WINS

The 6-0 triumph at Queens Park Rangers equalled the club record for a winning margin in an away league game and was also QPR's record home league defeat.

Sept 13th 2016

QPR 0-6 Newcastle United

Championship

Shelvey (2), Perez , Clark, Mitrovic, Hanley.

October 5th 1993

Notts County 1-7 Newcastle United

League Cup 2nd round, 2nd leg

(Aggregate 11-2)

Cole (3), Allen (2, 1p) Beardsley, Lee.§

September 29th 1962

Walsall 0-6 Newcastle United

Division Two

Fell, Kerray, Thomas (2), Suddick, Hilley.

February 1st 1932

Southport 0-9 Newcastle United

FA Cup 4th round, second replay – played at Hillsborough

Lang, McMenemy, Cape (2), Weaver, Boyd, JR Richardson (3)

September 10th 1927

Manchester United 1-7 Newcastle United

Division 1

Seymour (2), McDonald, Gallacher, Moore O.G., Urwin, Harris

October 26th 1912

Everton 0-6 Newcastle United

Division 1

Stewart (2), McTavish (2), Low (2)

March 28th 1908

Fulham 0-6 Newcastle United

Semi-final - played at Anfield

Appleyard, Gardner, Howie (2), Rutherford (2)

CHAPTER 7

WANDERING

As 'blips' go this one was hardly disastrous. It even included a win in a three game 'blip', but nonetheless the shock defeat at home to Wolves and a draw at Villa were the only games not won in a run of 18 fixtures.

NEWCASTLE UNITED 0 WOLVERHAMPTON WANDERERS 2

St. James'

Saturday 17th September 2016

SCORERS:
Mbemba O.G.   29   0-1
Helder Costa   62   0-2

The biggest crowd of the season so far pitched up to see The Toon continue to sweep all before them. Managed by Italy's Italia '90 World Cup goalkeeper Walter Zenga, Wolves had started the season reasonably well but had collapsed to a 4-0 home defeat against Barnsley as Newcastle were hammering QPR.

While many turned up expecting Wolves to be given the same treatment, football being football the formbook was turned on its head leaving Benitez to point out in his post-match assessment, "When I said the other day there was plenty of room for improvement I think some people were surprised but you can see now we need to improve".

Portuguese starlet Helder Costa proved to be the thorn in the side of a Magpies line-up showing four change to the mid-week XI. Just before the half hour mark Chancel Mbemba put through his own goal in desperately trying to prevent Costa from scoring but the former Benfica and Monaco man wasn't to be denied and duly doubled the lead with a magnificently curling shot two thirds of the way into a match that definitely didn't go according to plan.

The flow of the game wasn't helped by more flourishing of cards than on a night out with Paul Daniels. Five Wanderers players found their way into the book as did Paul Dummett, Mo Diame and Matt Ritchie with Vurnon Anita receiving one of the red variety with a couple of minutes remaining on what was a disappointing afternoon all round.

Further disappointment would follow a month and a half later when it belatedly emerged that Jonjo Shelvey had been charged over alleged use of abusive language to Wolves Moroccan player Romain Saiss. Although Shelvey pleaded not guilty he would duly be fined £100,000 and banned for five matches.

UNITED: Sels, Anita, Mbemba, Lascelles, Dummett, Ritchie (Atsu 63), Shelvey, Hayden (Mitrovic 63), Perez, Diame, Gayle.

Unused: Darlow, Yedlin, Clark, Colback, Gouffran

Attendance: 52,117

Referee: Tim Robinson

Post-match league position: 3rd

NEWCASTLE UNITED 2 WOLVERHAMPTON WANDERERS 0

St. James'

Tuesday 20th September 2016

EFL Cup 3rd round

SCORERS:

Ritchie	29	1-0
Gouffran	31	2-0

As moments of déjà vu go this wasn't quite what it might seem. While the two clubs lined up once again at St. James' a mere three days after they had last met, each manager made eight changes with Newcastle asking only Shelvey, Diame and Ritchie to start both games. Debuts were handed to Lazaar and Murphy while Yedlin had a starting place for the first time.

While the line ups were much changed those in the crowd of just under 35,000 witnessed something akin to what they'd expected at the weekend as United rained in 20 efforts on goal. Only four of those were on target with two goals scored without reply but with no goal difference to strengthen it was good enough even if the score-line should have been wider, Diame's chip that struck the bar being the nearest of the near misses.

United went ahead in the same minute that they fell behind in at the weekend, Matt Ritchie side-footing home after trading passes with Jack Colback for his first goal other than the penalty against Reading.

As in the previous round Newcastle struck twice in two minutes – albeit there was the small matter of half time in between the two goals against Cheltenham. This time having got on the score-sheet himself Ritchie turned provider but all the credit had to go to the goal-scorer as Yoan Gouffran met Matt's cross full on the volley.

Newcastle were to be first out of the hat again when the draw was made for the next round, Preston destined to be the visitors but there were half a dozen league games to navigate before then and for all the fans' frustration over the lack of cup ambition in recent years, this season's absolute number one target was to spend as little time as possible in the Championship and so the cup could be seen as a bonus, but one that could wait.

UNITED: Darlow, Yedlin, Hanley, Clark, Lazaar, Ritchie (Lascelles 86), Shelvey, Colback, Gouffran (Atsu 74), Diame (Perez 72), Murphy.

Unused: Woodman, Dummett, Hayden Mitrovic.

Att: 34,735

Referee: Andy Woolmer

ASTON VILLA 1   NEWCASTLE UNITED 1

Villa Park

Saturday 24th September 2016

SCORERS:

Elphick O.G.	**28**	**1-0**
Tshibola	88	1-1

Looking to bounce back into the Premier League at the first attempt having installed a Champions League winning manager and investing substantially in the team wasn't just Newcastle United's plan. The same approach had been taken at Aston Villa where Roberto Di Matteo was in charge.

Struggling to adapt to their new surroundings following relegation, Villa's solitary win had come at home to Rotherham, the side destined to be marooned at the foot of the table. It wasn't how things had been foreseen at Villa Park and 2012 Champions League winner Di Matteo was sacked two games later following a defeat at Preston. Villa's travails only illustrate how Rafa Benitez's achievement in taking the Toon up should never be taken for granted, but appreciated for how smoothly the Rafalution was carried out.

At Villa Park United led for an hour after taking the lead thanks to an own goal at almost exactly the same point of the game an O.G. had put them ahead in mid-week. This time though United weren't able to extend the lead and eventually paid the price when Villa got a late equaliser to tie up their fourth game in a row.

Decent in the first half when former Bournemouth man Tommy Elphick put through his own goal from a Yedlin cross, United had good shouts for a penalty waved away by referee Chris Kavanagh shortly afterwards when Dwight Gayle appeared to be fouled.

As the game became scrappy in the second half Cheick Tiote came on for what would prove to be his final league appearance but he was powerless to stop Aaron Tshibola's late leveller from a Jordan Ayew corner.

Coming on the back of the defeat in the previous league game, Newcastle remained outside the automatic promotion places as Norwich leap-frogged Huddersfield to top the table ahead of their visit to Tyneside four days later.

UNITED: Sels, Yedlin (Tiote 75), Lascelles, Clark, Dummett, Ritchie, Hayden, Shelvey, Gouffran, Diame, Gayle (Mitrovic 80).

Unused: Darlow, Hanley, Lazaar, Perez, Atsu

Attendance: 32,062

Referee: Chris Kavanagh

Post-match league position: 5th

Chapter 8

AFTER-BURNERS

It had been a decent start to the season despite that false start of the opening two defeats. United had got into their stride before the single point from the disappointing home defeat by Wolves and the draw at Villa. Even that blip had been punctuated by a League Cup stroll against Wolves and Newcastle were about to turn on the after-burners and invite the rest of the Championship to catch us if you can.

NEWCASTLE UNITED 4   NORWICH CITY 3

St. James'

Wednesday 28th September 2016

SCORERS:

Gayle	**24**	**1-0**
Dorrans	44p	1-1
Jerome	52	1-2
Murphy	69	1-3
Gayle	**71**	**2-3**
Gouffran	**90+5**	**3-3**
Gayle	**90+6**	**4-3**

Only the most mercenary footballers would think this and Paul Dummett certainly isn't one of those, but when he came off two minutes into injury time the Wales international must have thought the birthday presents he had received two days earlier would be the only gifts he'd be receiving this week. However, just four minutes later United had won a game they'd been losing when Dummett came off.

At least Paul was able to enjoy the transformation, many of the paying public had drifted off to drown their sorrows only to miss one of the legendary fight-backs as Newcastle overcame Norwich to move within a point of them, albeit Huddersfield's win over Rotherham 24 hours earlier had already pushed The Canaries off their perch at the top of the table, and of more concern had dropped The Toon down to ninth.

Newcastle should have won in a canter. Dwight Gayle's goal that had given United the advantage mid-way through the first half was scant reward for peppering Michael McGovern's goal. It had been hoped that the horrible habit of conceding just before half time had been stamped out but against the run of play the high-flying Canaries drew level when Yoan Gouffran made what was definitely a forward's tackle in the box to bring down Robbie Brady, leaving Graham Dorrans with the task of sending Karl Darlow the wrong way from the spot.

Duly boosted, Norwich came out looking like a different team to the one seen earlier. They went ahead seven minutes into the second half when Cameron Jerome curled in a shot from the left hand side of the box, and when Jacob Murphy's deflected effort extended the visitors' lead with just 21 minutes to play it looked like the points were on their way back to East Anglia.

Gayle would go home with the match ball. The 26 year-old scored the first and last goals of the game but arguably it was his middle strike that was the most important. Coming just two minutes after the only two goal margin in the match was opened up, Gayle got The Lads straight back into the contest, and what a goal it was. Jonjo Shelvey's range of passing was already proving to be one of the most dangerous weapons in the Tyneside armoury and the Londoner hit a pin-point ball further than some people go for their holidays. Good as it was the pass took some controlling but Gayle took the wind out of it with a sublime first touch, clinically finishing with his second. There was no time for celebrations as Gayle quickly grabbed the ball and got it back to the centre-circle for the re-start.

Newcastle kept trying to get the equaliser but to all intents and purposes it looked as if Norwich had the experience and know-how to simply see the game out and pocket the points that would take them back to the top of the table. Football is the great theatre it is though because as well as moments of great talent, such as Gayle's second goal, you never know quite how the drama is going to end. There was certainly drama to be had on this evening under the lights at St. James'. Paul Dummett had shaken hands, taken his trackie top and sat down when suddenly the sting in the tail turned the match on its head.

Having given away the penalty that let Norwich back into the game Yoan Gouffran suddenly scored out of next to nothing, turning in a header from a DeAndre Yedlin cross to make it 3-3. The goal was not in keeping with the screamers Gouffran had previously come up with but it was as important as any and made more so when moments later Gayle sensationally latched onto a ball on the edge of the box and fired in a low shot, which having failed to keep out, 'keeper McGovern will have had nightmares about for weeks.

The late, late come-back made this a high-point in a season of highs. Even the normally restrained Rafa admitted, "I did a little fist pump. Normally I am calm", adding "To feel the fans here when you are scoring goals and winning the game was amazing."

UNITED: Darlow, Yedlin, Lascelles, Clark, Dummett (Atsu 90+2), Ritchie, Shelvey, Colback (Hayden 71), Gouffran, Diame (Mitrovic 71) Gayle.

Unused: Sels, Lazaar, Mbemba, Perez,

Attendance: 48,236

Referee: Peter Bankes

Post-match league position: 3rd

ROTHERHAM UNITED 0 NEWCASTLE UNITED 1

New York Stadium

Saturday 1st October 2016

SCORER:

Atsu	41	1-0

This was a classic case of a team raising their game against The Toon but The Toon coming through. The not so merry Millers had a beast of a season. Having won just one of their 11 league games before Newcastle's visit, this game was the middle match of seven successive defeats before a draw at Ipswich offered momentary respite before four more reverses.

Already cemented to the foot of the table Rotherham would only sink deeper and deeper into the mire as the season progressed but when Newcastle arrived at the New York Stadium the home side scrapped like a bruiser in the Bronx.

Christian Atsu may well have had an enjoyable few days playing on the fact that in the four minutes he played against Norwich, United came from a goal down to win. Whatever his contribution against Norwich the on loan Chelsea man proved to be the match-winner here on his first start for the club. Picking up a pass from Jonjo Shelvey shortly before the break, Atsu cut in to curl home a shot out of keeping with the rest of the game but one that proved Benitez's final whistle assessment, as the gaffer explained, "The game plan was to work hard and do our best in terms of physicality and tempo and then after that use your quality. That is what we did."

It had been anything but easy though as the basement side twice hit the bar through John Taylor and Dominic Ball but as at Bristol City a clean sheet and a moment of magic was all that was needed to take maximum reward, the building momentum seeing Newcastle perched a point behind second placed Norwich who won a late kick-off to edge The Toon off a second placed occupied for just a couple of hours.

UNITED: Darlow, Anita, Lascelles, Clark, Dummett, Atsu (Ritchie 67), Shelvey, Colback, Gouffran, Diame (Hanley 87) Gayle (Mitrovic 79)

Unused: Sels, Hayden, Mbemba, Yedlin

Attendance: 11,653

Referee: Roger East

Post-match league position: 3rd

NEWCASTLE UNITED 3 BRENTFORD 1

St. James'

Saturday 15th October 2016

SCORERS:

Clark	**11**	**1-0**
Gayle	**16**	**2-0**
Gayle	**49**	**3-0**
Hogan	52	3-1

The Bees were in fine fettle when they came north looking to buzz before the biggest league gate they'd played to since 1946. Sitting fifth in the table, The Londoners had reached the play-offs the year before, having achieved the same placing in their first year after promotion from League One. They had scored nine goals in their previous two home games and although they had slipped up at Wolves on their last away trip, prior to that they had taken a point from Villa and won at Brighton, so were tricky opponents.

For all their pre-match confidence though The Bees weren't given the chance to settle and found themselves two down at St. James with barely quarter of an hour gone, eventually being beaten 3-1.

Perhaps it might have been more awkward for United had the visitors' top scorer Scott Hogan not headed over from a good position early on. By the time he did find the back of the net in the second half the game was effectively over as Newcastle added three more points at a canter. Hogan would play at St. James' again later in the season after a big money move to Villa.

Dean Smith's side fell behind to a simple goal after 11 minutes as another man with a Villa connection, Ciaran Clark, made easy work of heading home a cross from Jonjo Shelvey. Within five minutes Dwight

Gayle doubled the lead to put United into cruise control although a killer third goal took its time arriving, Ayoze Perez seeing a 'goal' disallowed for offside and Christian Atsu missing a good opportunity to score for a second successive match.

Four minutes after the re-start Gayle's second rubber-stamped the three points and put himself out in front as the championship's leading scorer. Hogan reduced the deficit shortly afterwards but there was only one winner on an afternoon when a satisfied Benitez noted, "We did everything we wanted to, we controlled the game."

Victory took The Magpies back into the automatic promotion spots above Huddersfield who didn't play until the following day. Norwich topped the table after a home win over bottom of the table Rotherham but with Brighton dropping points at home to Preston and fifth and sixth placed Bristol City and Birmingham City having both lost the night before, a nice gap was opening up.

Suddenly United had a five-point advantage over the duo occupying the final play-off spots and with Huddersfield losing at home to Sheffield Wednesday 24 hours later it had been a good weekend. There was no time to reflect on that though as the relentless demands of the championship meant it was off to Barnsley the following Tuesday night and focus had to be paramount. Nothing was won yet with the ever alert Benitez stressing, "I'm not watching the table because it is too soon."

UNITED: Darlow, Anita, Lascelles (Hanley 60), Clark, Dummett, Atsu (Yedlin 72), Shelvey, Colback, Gouffran (Lazaar 84), Perez, Gayle.

Unused: Sels, Hayden, Diame, Mitrovic

Attendance: 51,885

Referee: Simon Hooper

Post-match league position: 2nd

BARNSLEY 0 NEWCASTLE UNITED 2

Oakwell,

Tuesday 18th October

SCORERS:

Gayle	49	1-0
Gayle	68	2-0

It's a pity the journey home wasn't longer as the Toon Army savoured that top of the table feeling for the first time following Dwight Gayle's two goal demolition job on The Tykes make it 12 points out of 12 and seven goals in his last four games for the striker.

Over five and a half thousand travelling fans in Oakwell's biggest gate of the season had to wait until the second half with the first goal coming in the same minute that the final one of the three against Brentford had been netted. It doesn't matter when the goals go in though as long as they do and with Gayle in blistering form, his first four minutes after the break with another mid-way through the half to allow Newcastle to ease to victory. Indeed but for a good save from Adam Davies thwarting his late diving header Gayle would have had a second hat –trick of the season. No-one was too worried about that though, Rafa reckoning, "He is on fire now. He is happy and we're all happy."

Whereas Brentford had been in confident mood the previous weekend, newly promoted Barnsley's bright start, which had seen them in third place a month earlier, had taken a dive. Going into the match the South Yorkshire side had gleaned just a solitary point from their previous five outings.

UNITED: Darlow, Anita, Lascelles, Clark, Dummett, Shelvey, Hayden, Ritchie (Atsu 82), Diame (Colback 90+2), Gouffran, Gayle.

Unused: Sels, Yedlin, Lazaar, Perez, Mitrovic

Attendance: 18,597

Referee: Paul Tierney

Post-match league position: 1st

NEWCASTLE UNITED 3   IPSWICH TOWN. 0

St. James'

Saturday 22nd October.

SCORERS:

Perez	**1**	**1-0**
Perez	**73**	**2-0**
Ritchie	**78**	**3-0**

Struggling Ipswich came into a daunting trip to a buoyant St. James' having beaten Burton at Portman Road last time out in ending a five match winless run. Nonetheless the Tractor Boys' confidence was fragile and should have been shattered when Perez put United a goal up in the first minute without Ipswich touching the ball until they had to pick it out of the net.

To their credit and befitting a club once managed with distinction by Sir Bobby Robson, Ipswich stuck at it and never gave up despite the chasm in class. Just a goal to the good, as the match wore on, worries began to creep in that the visitors would sneak a late leveller, as had happened in the trip to Aston Villa the last time a league game hadn't been won. While table topping United dominated, ex Newcastle man Leon Best showed Ipswich were capable of offering a threat if they were allowed to get forward, Best hitting the bar with a left foot shot before half time. When Gayle was denied what seemed a stonewall spot kick when felled by 'keeper Bart Bialkowski it seemed as if despite the early goal United were in for an afternoon of frustration as they looked to wrap up the points.

Eventually though patience and persistence paid off, and like a cricket team who have plugged away looking for a wicket, once one came another soon followed. Matt Ritchie was involved in both. Firstly he supplied the cross from which Perez plundered his second of the match with a superb finish from 12 yards in the 73rd minute. Five minutes later Ritchie's mercurial left foot produced one of the moments of the season when Perez returned the compliment by providing the assist. A few minutes earlier The Scotland international had seen his volley fly narrowly wide but this time his effort gave Bialkowski no chance as the score-line belatedly began to reflect the pattern of play. "After the second goal we had more control" acknowledged Rafa. "It was easy at the end but you could see the difficulty we had at the start of the second half."

Perhaps Benitez benefitted from Sir Bobby's presence. The telling goals came either side of a 76th minute dedicated to applause for the legendary figure whose statue of course stands proudly outside the stadium.

UNITED: Darlow, Yedlin, Lascelles, Clark, Dummett, Ritchie, Colback, Shelvey (Hayden 83), Gouffran (Atsu 75), Perez, Gayle (Mitrovic 79).

Unused: Sels, Anita, Mbemba, Diame,

Attendance: 51,963

Referee: James Adcock

Post-match league position: 1st

NEWCASTLE UNITED 6   PRESTON NORTH END 0

EFL Cup, Fourth Round

St. James'

Tuesday 25th October

SCORERS:

Mitrovic	19	1-0
Diame	38	2-0
Ritchie	53p	3-0
Mitrovic	55	4-0
Diame	87	5-0
Perez	90	6-0

As in the previous round against Wolves the EFL Cup visit of once proud Preston provided back to back fixtures with the same opposition. Caught out by Wolves in the first game of that earlier double header, North End were walloped 6-0 in the League Cup prior to a more modest but ultimately more important victory over the same club – if not quite the same team – at Deepdale the following weekend.

Only in 1976 had Newcastle attracted a bigger gate in the League Cup than the 49,042 who turned up for this meeting with Preston who had won away to Premier League Bournemouth in the previous round. Back in '76 Wembley was the final destination on the cup trail and with this annihilation of the opposition, a big squad and confidence booming, more than one voice was heard to wonder about a trip down Wembley Way as United equalled their widest winning margin in the competition.

Rafa reloaded with seven changes from the weekend win over Ipswich but it made no difference to the fire-power on display and had any one of the two efforts from Christian Atsu or one from Isaac Hayden that hit the woodwork gone in, there would have been a goal for every one of those changes.

As it was there was no need to fret about the ones that got away as the net bulged often enough with Mo Diame getting his first goals for the club, Perez and Ritchie continuing where they left off against Ipswich and Aleksandar Mitrovic emphasising his claims to a regular place.

With nine changes of their own Preston fielded a side very different to their usual line-up and were further disrupted when reduced to 10 men when the score was 1-0 as Alan Browne was shown red for elbowing red-head Colback.

Mitro headed the all-important opener, getting on the end of a Ritchie free kick with just under 20 minutes played before having a hand in the second strike seven minutes before half time. It was from the Serb's cross that the ball broke to Diame who at last got on the score-sheet in what was his 12th appearance since his big money move from Hull.

Never one to be shy and retiring Mitrovic next came to the fore early in the second half when United were awarded a penalty. Despite Ritchie being the side's spot-kick specialist and also having been the man fouled he had to literally put the ball under his shirt to stop Mitro grabbing it, so desperate was the striker to score again. Mitrovic might have exploded had Matt not applied the finish but fortunately there was no mistake and fired up by the incident Mitrovic lashed in the goal of the game to make it 4-0 just two minutes later. Had he taken and converted the penalty no doubt the ball would have been up Mitrovic's shirt instead of Ritchie's as a prized possession but there would be no hat-trick although the scoring was far from over.

Former United man Paul Huntington's eyes lit up at the thought of a consolation goal on his return to Tyneside only for Matz Sels to produce a brilliant save from his header to ensure a clean sheet on a night when he had been largely redundant.

Some of the youngsters in the crowd had left by the time a tiring Preston were further punished. Diame gave himself a few minutes to search for his own hat-trick after notching his second of the game three minutes from time, before sub Perez popped up in the right place at the right time to secure a second 6-0 victory of the season.

On the same night Arsenal, Liverpool, Leeds and Hull joined United in progressing into the quarter-finals as had Southampton, West Ham and Manchester United 24 hours earlier. Newcastle were once again in exalted company but it was being in with the big boys on a regular league basis which was the primary target, so when the draw paired Newcastle away to Hull it was something to look forward to but there were more important fixtures to fulfil first.

UNITED: Sels, Yedlin, Mbemba, Hanley, Dummett (Anita 58), Ritchie (Perez 76), Hayden, Colback (Shelvey 32), Atsu, Diame, Mitrovic.

UNUSED: Darlow, Clark, Gouffran, Gayle.

Att: 49,042

Referee: Andy Madley

PRESTON NORTH END 1-2 NEWCASTLE UNITED

Deepdale

Saturday 29th October.

SCORERS:

Mitrovic	**59**	**1-0**
Mitrovic	**71**	**2-0**
Lascelles O.G.	90	2-1

Almost a thousand fans travelled for every goal Newcastle had scored in midweek, 5,714 in a gate of 20,724 quirkily giving North End their biggest gate since a 2010 cup-tie with Chelsea on the back of a 6-0 defeat!

Smarting after their EFL Cup humiliation four days earlier Preston made nine changes to their starting line-up, reverting to the side which had impressively won at Norwich in their last league game. Having also defeated Huddersfield in the fixture before that the home side were determined to show a different side (in more ways than one) to the heavily defeated cup line up, especially as their mid-week challenge had been reduced by a red card in the opening half hour.

Newcastle were to find this a demanding encounter but one where once again they demonstrated that under Benitez they had acquired the grit and determination to match the style and swagger that drew more accolades. Winning promotion requires coming through games like this with points on the board not hard-luck stories to tell.

United were under the cosh for much of this game, a fact illustrated by having just 44% possession and no corners. Nonetheless they established a hard won two goal advantage and then withstood a late barrage from the home side.

Newcastle made five changes from the mid-week triumph but were unable to call upon hamstring victim Gayle, leaving the way open for Mitrovic to pursue his claim for first team football.

Operating a 4-4-2 that got the ball forward early Simon Grayson's Preston showed they were a different proposition to their previous meeting with the visitors grateful to Jamaal Lascelles for clearing off the line from a first half Alex Baptiste header.

In an attritional encounter the first goal was always likely to be crucial. Two thirds of the game had elapsed when that goal went Newcastle's way, Aleksandar Mitrovic powering onto a ball played over the top to make the chance count with a clinical finish.

Soon afterwards Grayson was livid when no penalty was given as Callum Robinson went down under challenge from Ciaran Clark and the manager who succeeded Lee Clark as Huddersfield boss was apoplectic moments later as Newcastle doubled their advantage when Mitrovic was again the main man, this time turning in a DeAndre Yedlin cross.

It should have been plain sailing after that, but unlike on Tuesday night when Preston collapsed, conceding a couple of late goals that turned a heavy defeat into a record equalling one, this time more spiritedly before their own fans they reduced the deficit. Lascelles was pressurised into turning the ball into his own net from Greg Cunningham's cross to leave United hanging on through an extended period of added time.

If the home side felt aggrieved at the non-award of the earlier penalty shout that was nothing compared to the howls of anguish when Jermaine Beckford went down under challenge from the former skipper of West Lancashire derby rivals Grant Hanley. Referee Chris Kavanagh was unimpressed and waved play on but Newcastle still needed the woodwork to help them protect the lead as sub Marrick Vermijl still had time to hit the post.

The final whistle when it eventually came was a blessed relief but this victory was essentially more satisfying than the 6-0 win. Firstly this was because it meant three more points, and secondly the side had been made to face a much stiffer challenge away from home but once again had showed they were capable of meeting whatever obstacles were put in their way.

"They were pushing and pushing and we were defending. In the end the main thing was to get the three points and we did it" commented a delighted Benitez who as he got on the team bus shortly afterwards must have been delighted that his side had not buckled.

UNITED: Darlow, Yedlin (Hanley 90+5), Lascelles, Clark, Dummett, Ritchie (Atsu 90+2), Hayden, Shelvey, Gouffran, Diame, Mitrovic (Perez 86)

Unused: Sels, Lazaar, Anita, Gamez

Att: 20,724

Referee: Chris Kavanagh

Post-match league position: 1st

ALEKSANDAR'S RAG-TIME BAND

Message boards, phone-ins and pub talk all need fuel and the issue of whether Rafa should use Aleksandar Mitrovic or Dwight Gayle as his spearhead – or whether he should change the habits of a lifetime and play the two of them up front – was a constant source of debate. There could be no arguments with Gayle's inclusion whenever fit because of the former Crystal Palace man's goals but the young Serbian striker's advocates were also very vocal and who could blame them?

Mitrovic's match-winning performance at Preston came on the back of his only other starts being the 6-0 wins over both PNE and QPR, as well as the comfortable 2-0 cup win over Cheltenham when he'd had to be subbed before half time. He now tallied five goals in his other three starts including braces in both games against Preston despite not taking that cup penalty! Add to that a two goal salvo for Serbia in a World Cup qualifier against Austria in his most recent international appearance and the 22 year old wasn't so much knocking on Senor Benitez's door as knocking it off its hinges. "Mitrovic has given me a very good problem to have" smiled Rafa after the win at Preston.

Mitrovic would start the following weekend's win over Cardiff and his next goal would be against Welsh opposition – albeit for Serbia v Wales a week after that. His next goal for United wouldn't come until a February winner at Wolves but with his passion, energy and determination Mitro would maintain his army of admirers and show signs of calming the effervescent element of his self-control, cards becoming rarer and paler.

NEWCASTLE UNITED 2 CARDIFF CITY 1

St. James'

Saturday 5th November

SCORERS:

Atsu	3	1-0
Gouffran	45	2-0
Whittingham	77	2-1

With visitors from South Wales it was perhaps appropriate that all three goals came from throw-ins. This wasn't the greatest of games by any stretch of the imagination and some of the blame or credit for that – depending upon your point of view – should probably go to Bluebirds boss Neil Warnock whose side managed to restrict United's fluency regardless of the boost of yet another early goal, and the fact that Newcastle had the ball for two-thirds of the game.

Just over a couple of minutes had elapsed when a Paul Dummett throw led to the quick break-through. Receiving possession Mitrovic traded passes with Perez. It seemed as everyone in the ground expected Mitro to shoot, especially with the pressure of fit again Gayle sitting on the bench, ready if needed only for the Serbian to surprise maybe even himself when he laid the ball off for Atsu to accept the gift and open the scoring. In for the suspended Ritchie, Atsu was the solitary change to the team who had won at Preston as Rafa's rotation slowed.

Yoan Gouffran hadn't scored since the dramatic denouement against

Norwich but the Frenchman made half-time a lot more enjoyable than it might have been by doubling the lead on the stroke of half-time, again the move starting with a Dummett throw.

After the break though the killer third goal just wouldn't come, Atsu and Mitrovic passing up the most inviting opportunities and Newcastle's seventh successive league victory looked in jeopardy when from another throw- in Peter Whittingham halved the deficit with 13 minutes to go.

Unlike the previous week at Preston, the opponents were unable to put United under any sustained pressure and the clock wound down without too much worry. Not every game could be a six-nil slaughter or a seven goal thriller but the important thing was that three more points were added to the tally.

Possibly some of the day's highlights came before the match actually started thanks to a spectacular flag display honouring a dozen club legends on a day when the famous black and white shirts also included a splash of red in the form of a poppy to mark the forthcoming Remembrance weekend.

UNITED: Darlow, Yedlin, Lascelles, Clark, Dummett, Atsu (Diame 89), Shelvey, Hayden, Gouffran (Anita 72), Perez, Mitrovic.

Unused: Sels, Lazaar, Hanley, Colback, Gayle.

Attendance: 51,257

Referee: Tony Harrington

Post-match league position: 1st

LEEDS UNITED 0 NEWCASTLE UNITED 2

Sunday 20th November

SCORERS:

Gayle	23	1-0
Gayle	54	2-0

Something had to give as the Uniteds went into this game having won their last three and last eight games respectively. Something that didn't give was a togetherness that regardless of past rivalries brought fans of both clubs together in the 11th minute as applause rang around the ground in honour of Gary Speed as the fifth anniversary of his tragically early death approached.

A sold out crowd of marginally over 36,000 squeezed into Elland Road making it Leeds' biggest home game of the season and the highest gate Newcastle played in front of away from home throughout the promotion campaign.

Those in attendance were accompanied by those enjoying their Sunday lunches while taking in the game live on Sky. They saw that while Garry Monk's side were full of endeavour that was matched by The Magpies who could also call upon that all important extra quality.

Having been out of the Premier League since 2004 Leeds lacked the number of household names they once commanded but in ex England goalkeeper Rob Green they had someone of the sort of stature they were used to when they were winning trophies and contesting European finals. Green it was though who committed a ridiculous error of judgement to hand Newcastle the lead mid-way through the first half. With an over-hit long searching ball from Jack Colback coming to earth just in front of his goal Green had the simple task of tipping it over the top for a corner. Instead, even though he knew Gayle was prowling Green decided to catch it only to treat the ball as if it had been covered in soap and palm it down to the feet of Gayle who gleefully accepted the gift for his easiest goal of the campaign.

At the other end Karl Darlow; on his way to his sixth clean sheet in his 10th match of the season so far, showed how to deal competently with relatively simple situations by tipping Luke Ayling's header over the top when Leeds threatened.

Having had a fortunate hand in the first goal Jack Colback was involved when the lead was doubled before Leeds could attempt to get up a head of steam after the break when he combined with Perez before Vurnon Anita delivered a cross which invited Gayle to plunder another goal from close range.

Victory took the points tally to 40 from 17 games, despite losing the opening pair. Equalling the club record of nine consecutive wins inevitably saw a gap opening up with second placed Brighton now five points behind and Leeds fully 14 points adrift, one place outside the play-off berths. Leeds would end up refunding their season ticket holders for failing to secure at least a place in the end of season lottery but for Newcastle in time it would be an immediate return to the top flight after a single season sabbatical. For that the Toon Army should recognise that regardless of history and fan-base, membership of the top flight cannot be taken for granted and Rafa's achievement in immediately guiding the club back to the promised land is one which quite possibly would not have been achieved without him.

Typically of a confident and assured leader, Benitez himself was looking to share the credit and with that continue to get the best out of everyone around him. "I have to say thanks to every player" he said. "We could see a performance today against a good team. We saw the effort, the mentality was good and the understanding of the game was very good."

UNITED: Darlow, Anita, Lascelles, Clark, Dummett, Ritchie, Colback (Hayden 83), Shelvey, Gouffran (Diame 76), Perez, Gayle (Mitrovic 79).

Unused: Sels, Yedlin, Mbemba,Atsu.

Att: 36,002

Referee: Graham Scott

Post-match league position: 1st

The day before the home game with lowly Blackburn was a month to the day before Christmas, but The Toon Army felt as if Christmas had already arrived as the previous weekend's win over Leeds was the ninth in a row. Starting with that late-late come-back against Norwich, United had stormed to the top of the table and reached the quarter-finals of the League Cup. If only football was always like this. Even the most inexperienced fan knew that not every game could be won but at this stage of the season it seemed that whatever obstacles were put in their way, United would find a solution.

CHAPTER 9

MID-SEASON MIXTURE

NEWCASTLE UNITED 0   BLACKBURN ROVERS 1

St. James'

Saturday 26th November 2016

SCORERS:
Mulgrew   75   0-1

"I didn't like our reaction when we were losing, and we have to do a lot better. I didn't like the chances we didn't take, and I didn't like my decisions."

In an era when football managers are quick to blame officials, underhand methods of the opposition, the pitch markings not being straight enough or the ball boys not having the right colour socks on, it was refreshing to see Rafa take his own share of the responsibility for a shock defeat by struggling Rovers.

Maybe over-confidence was the problem as United made six changes ahead of a game which would have seen a club record 10th successive victory had things gone to plan. Only two subs were used, one of the replacements, Jesus Gamez, stretchered off on his full league debut. Having fallen behind in the 75th minute it was surprising that Gayle did not come on until the 85th while goal threats Diame and Gouffran remained unused options.

If the talk in The Strawberry was why didn't Rafa change it more with his subs or for that matter why did he change it so much from the start, then Benitez was evidently asking himself he same questions as he brushed his teeth before bed-time.

However the gaffer shouldn't have been too hard on himself, after all the previous nine games had been won. With United in pole position in the table the changes had evidently been made with one eye on the approaching mid-week EFL Cup quarter-final at Hull. For years fans had grumbled about the club not taking the cups seriously but serial trophy winner Rafa looked to be keeping some cards up his sleeve.

In two months' time a much changed United would be humbled in the FA Cup at League One Oxford to the consternation of many while here there appeared to be a balancing act attempted between league and cup.

It simply wasn't United's day as Rovers won with one of their two on target efforts from a meagre 34% possession. The problem was Newcastle only gave Rovers' 'keeper Jason Steele the same number of on target efforts to deal with, even though seven minutes of added time gave United the opportunity to throw the kitchen sink at Owen Coyle's side's rear-guard.

Rovers stunned another big gate with quarter of an hour left, from a corner with ex Celtic man Charlie Mulgrew volleying home a goal worthy of winning a game – just preferably not this one.

Losing to Rovers had unfortunately become a bad habit as this was the sixth time they had won on their last seven league visits to Tyneside.

UNITED: Darlow, Yedlin, Mbemba (Gayle 85), Clark, Gamez (Dummett 55), Ritchie, Hayden, Shelvey, Atsu, Perez, Mitrovic

Unused: Sels, Lascelles, Anita, Diame, Gouffran

Attendance: 52.092

Referee: David Coote

Post-match league position: 1st

HULL CITY 1   NEWCASTLE UNITED 1

(lost 1-3 on penalties)

KCOM Stadium

EFL Cup quarter-final

Tuesday 29th November 2016

SCORERS:

Diame	**98**	**1-0**
Snodgrass	99	1-1

PENALTY SHOOT OUT

Shelvey	**saved**	**0-0**
Snodgrass	scored	0-1
Gayle	**hit bar**	**0-1**
Dawson	scored	0-2
Atsu	**scored**	**1-2**
Huddleston	scored	1-3
Gouffran	**saved**	**1-3**

Newcastle had every chance to move into what would have been a two-legged semi-final with one of the big boys. Had they done so then the prospect of a double-header with either Liverpool, Southampton or Manchester United; who Hull themselves actually drew, would have whetted the appetite for a Premier League return. However given the anticipation before this match maybe the prospect of a prestigious semi-final could have provided an unwanted distraction from the relentless march back to the top-flight? It didn't seem like a good thing on the night, but with the benefit of hindsight Benitez's focus on the main prize was always by far the most important target. Now that Newcastle are back in the big league they can have a real go at bringing silverware to the north-east.

Struggling in the bottom three of the Premier League Hull had won just one of their previous 11 league games but had beaten the City's of Bristol, Stoke and Exeter in the EFL Cup.

Newcastle played in all white but this was no surrender as they were the better side but just couldn't find a way through in normal time: Gayle, Ritchie, Hayden and former Hull man Diame all having chances.

Evidently not fancying extra time ahead of their forthcoming six-pointer at Middlesbrough, Hull boss Mike Phelan made a triple-substitution 11 minutes from time. Nonetheless Phelan found his side having to expend extra energy in the additional 30 minutes when Dieumerci Mbokani stupidly got himself sent off in the 89th minute, after a clash with Jamaal Lascelles. Maybe Mbokani didn't fancy the extra-time himself?

With a man advantage and the door to the last four open it seemed a matter of time until Newcastle booked their place in the semi-finals of this competition for the first time since 1976. Achraf Lazaar hit the bar while Ciaran Clark and Jonjo Shelvey threatened before Diame deflated his former fans by finishing off a short corner.

One nil up against 10 tiring men in a game where they had been the better side, what could possibly go wrong for Newcastle? Well, possibly thinking the game was over as they switched off and let Hull straight back into the match barely a minute later. Former Spurs centre-half Michael Dawson launched the sort of long ball that would bring howls of derision at White Hart Lane but United couldn't deal with it, leaving Matz Sels to fail to collect a shot from sub Marcus Henriksen allowing Hull's most cultured player, Robert Snodgrass, to bring parity after the parry.

Despite bringing on two sets of fresh legs in the second half of extra time United were unable to force a winner in the remaining 21 minutes and so Newcastle were left with the prospect of a penalty shoot–out. While the last such conclusion had been won at Watford a decade earlier, Newcastle's previous penalty record had seen a 100% loss rate from eight attempts and that dismal record would continue as the away side's spot-kicks were woeful. Only sub Atsu had the composure to score from the spot while Hull only needed to take three of their kicks to win.

"It is a pity when you play so well and go out" reflected Rafa but the journey home seemed longer than the 143 miles it is on a night when it was a case of so near and yet so far.

UNITED: Sels, Anita (Yedlin 109), Lascelles, Clark, Lazaar, Ritchie (Atsu 81), Shelvey, Hayden (Murphy 105), Gouffran, Diame, Gayle. Unused: Darlow, Dummett, Mbemba, Tiote

Att: 16,243

Referee: Neil Swarbrick

NOTTINGHAM FOREST 2   NEWCASTLE UNITED 1

City Ground

Friday 2nd December 2016

SCORERS:

Ritchie	**45**	**1-0**
Bendtner	52	1-1
Lascelles O.G.	86	1-2

As December began The Chuckle Brothers were starring in Panto at Nottingham Theatre Royal, but it was at The City Ground on the night of Newcastle's visit that 'Oh no it isn't' seemed to be the call as referee Steve Martin produced a performance his American comedian namesake would have been proud of.

Starring as the dame in the City Ground rival to the nearby Nottingham stage, Forest's Henri Lansbury set himself up as the target for the Toon Army's booing but those who laugh last laugh longest. While Lansbury missed Forest's return to St. James' later the same month, shortly afterwards he would appear on Tyneside with Villa and shuffle the ball into his own net.

Forest were in good form going into this televised game, the Tricky Trees coming into the match on the back of successive away wins, having scored five at Barnsley last time out. For Newcastle it was imperative to get back on track after the disappointments of the last week.

Operating in a 3-5-1-1 shape Philippe Montanier's Forest welcomed back old boys Karl Darlow and Jamaal Lascelles, but the pair were to experience vastly different returns. Darlow would save two penalties – making people wonder how his inclusion at Hull might have changed the outcome – while Lascelles unfortunately put a late winner through his own net.

Having struggled through conceding goals just before half time in the early part of the season Newcastle got the boost of a goal on the cusp of the break for the second time in four games, as Ritchie rifled home Hayden's supply line from the left. To say Newcastle needed that advantage would be an understatement as while they went in a goal up they also went in two men down!

Jonjo Shelvey had found his evening curtailed just 33 minutes after it started when referee Martin brandished his red card for the first time. Adjudged to have fouled Lansbury Shelvey was sent off only for Karl Darlow to save from Nicklas Bendtner, a man who had previously scored from the spot against United in a derby match.

A good looking 'goal' from Ciaran Clark was mysteriously disallowed before Forest were given another chance to score from the spot in first-half injury time when once again Lansbury dissolved under challenge. Shelvey might have wondered where the rest of the team were if he was sat in the dressing room when Paul Dummett walked in but Dummett had received the game's second red card. When the rest of the players arrived shortly afterwards Darlow had the tale to tell of how he'd saved the spot-kick, this time Lansbury himself having failed with his kick.

If Benitez had plenty to say at the interval imagine what was being said across the corridor in the dressing room once dominated by Brian Clough. A goal down to nine men, Forest knew that if they failed to come back and win they would never be allowed to forget it. As for the conversation in the officials' room who knows how the game's big moments were being considered.

Forest started the second half with defender Michael Mancienne replaced by Britt Assombalonga, the powerful but injury plagued striker. Newcastle needed to hold out and frustrate the home side for as long as possible but just seven minutes after the re-start Bendtner bundled in an equaliser, leaving the final whistle looking a long way away for the nine men.

Somehow Newcastle managed to even fashion a couple of efforts on goal, Gayle firing in a shot from outside the box mid-way through the half, and Hayden shooting wide 12 minutes from time. Such respite was overdue to an over-worked defence manfully keeping out the full strength home side, whose fans were becoming increasingly restless at their inability to find a way through the depleted United.

Eventually fatigue would take its toll and like a marathon runner collapsing 100 yards from the finishing line Newcastle fell behind with 88 minutes on the clock. Distracted by the lurking Assombalonga, Jamaal Lascelles marked his return to the City Ground by inadvertently deflecting Apostolos Vellios's ball into the box beyond the despairing Darlow.

Defeat meant back to back reverses for the first time since the false start in the opening two games and with a cup exit in between it had been a bad week to say the least.

Newcastle had been on the receiving end of two reds, three yellows and two penalties compared to the home side's two yellows despite Forest committing seven more fouls. What mattered now would be how they reacted. Subsequent appeals against both red cards were quickly upheld with potential suspensions for two important players quashed, but the damage on the night had been done where instead of a likely three points United got none.

UNITED: Darlow, Yedlin, Lascelles, Clark, Dummett, Hayden, Shelvey, Ritchie, Perez (Anita 45), Gouffran (Diame 77), Gayle (Mitrovic 87).

Unused: Sels, Mbemba, Tiote, Atsu

Attendance: 21,317

Referee: Steve Martin

Post-match league position: 1st

NEWCASTLE UNITED 4 BIRMINGHAM CITY 0

St. James'

Saturday 10th December 2016

SCORERS:

Gayle	18	1-0
Gayle	24	2-0
Gouffran	47	3-0
Gayle	77	4-0

Birmingham City became the innocent fall guys of United's reaction to a robbery Robin Hood would have been embarrassed by. In a Play Off place when they arrived at Newcastle, The Blues had lost badly at home to Barnsley the previous weekend but had won at Brentford and drawn at Huddersfield in their two previous away games and were expected to offer more resistance than they did in fact muster.

Much of this was down to the fact that Newcastle had had eight days of fulminating over the injustice of the loss at Forest, not to mention the frustration of the shoot-out cup elimination, and that somehow they had conspired to lose to Blackburn the last time they'd appeared in front of the home fans.

By mid-way through the first half any nerves had been settled and Gayle was on a hat-trick. By full time the advantage had been doubled and Dwight had another match ball to put on the mantelpiece, although this one came without any of the drama the hat-trick against Norwich had produced.

Instead this was a nice, even easy, taking apart of a side near the top of the table. It signified that any wobble in form was over and done with and Newcastle were back on track.

Whereas being on TV on the Friday night of the week before had given others an incentive after Newcastle's defeat at Forest, on this occasion Newcastle kicked off in the knowledge that Brighton had leap-frogged them by beating Leeds the night before. If Brighton hoped that might put pressure on Newcastle they were about to find out that United thrived on it. After all Rafa the Gaffer was used to much bigger games than Birmingham at home and Newcastle looked at ease right from the kick off. "I think the first half we played really well and had a lot of chances" he said later, adding, "We played attacking football with some pace and good situations that we practiced. The players were enjoying it."

They weren't the only ones as another crowd of over 52,000 found that in not bothering with the Christmas shopping they'd found the gifts were all on offer against the men from St. Andrews. With 20 shots on goal and half of them on target there wasn't too much chance of getting cold, unless you were Karl Darlow trying to keep warm at the other end.

A bright start was rewarded with a rare header from Dwight Gayle to open the scoring. A more likely right footed finish from the same player doubled the lead six minutes later, Mo Diame having had a hand in both goals.

Two-nil was modest reward for a scintillating first half but that was soon rectified when the newly blonde haired Yoan Gouffran netted soon after the re-start to allow the score-line to more accurately reflect the play, and simultaneously squash any hopes the visitors might have had of getting back into the game.

Remaining in cruise control Newcastle made it 4-0 with Gayle's hat-trick goal 13 minutes from time. Two minutes later he was given a standing ovation as Rafa took him off with the job well and truly done, that final left footed finish giving Gayle a classic hat-trick.

With the same referee who had overseen the 6-0 win at QPR surely someone must have been tempted to ask Santa if United could have this ref every week.

Beaten manager Gary Rowett wasn't blaming the referee but someone was blaming him. "It was a bit of a football lesson. It was also an athletic lesson" conceded the Blues boss. He was to discover how football can hand out undeserved lessons when he was very surprisingly sacked four days later. In mid-March he would replace Steve McClaren at Derby County and within a month see his new side defeat Birmingham on their own patch. Having been sacked when they were seventh, Rowett would see Birmingham struggle to survive by a single point on the final day. He had made way for big name managers in Gianfranco Zola and subsequently Harry Redknapp. The lesson that ultimately needed learning was that it is not having a big name manager that matters, it's having a good one. Clearly in Benitez Newcastle have one of the best.

UNITED: Darlow, Anita, Lascelles, Clark, Dummett, Ritchie, Shelvey, Hayden (Lazaar 82), Gouffran (Atsu 70), Diame, Gayle. (Mitrovic 79)

Unused: Sels, Mbemba, Yedlin, Tiote

Attendance: 52,145

Referee: Andy Davies

Post-match league position: 1st

WIGAN ATHLETIC 0 NEWCASTLE UNITED 2

DW Stadium

Wednesday 14th December 2016

SCORERS:

Diame	26	1-0
Atsu	78	2-0

The visit of Newcastle was just what Wigan didn't need, other than for the financial boost of their biggest crowd of the season so far, regardless of it being a mid-week match. Under Warren Joyce, The Latics were only being kept off the bottom of the table by no-hopers Rotherham. They would still be in the drop zone at the end of the campaign (Though Joyce had since departed) having never escaped the bottom three. However only a fortnight earlier they had sprung a surprise by winning at Huddersfield and with United having lost on seven of their last eight visits and with recent experience of losing to struggling teams this was a test of United's mentality. A professional job was what was required to return to the top of the table following Brighton's win over Blackburn earlier.

Senegal international Mo Diame had often been something of a peripheral figure since his move from Hull at the start of the season but he had been outstanding against Birmingham despite Gayle obviously hogging the headlines with his hat-trick. Here though the former Wigan man pushed himself to the fore scoring his first league goal after bursting from the half way line before picking his spot after trading passes with Hayden.

While never anywhere near as fluent as against Birmingham (despite the first unchanged line-up of the campaign), Newcastle always had a degree of control, keeping Wigan at bay despite the home side having a fair bit of the ball but rarely threatening. Any hopes Wigan had of mounting a late surge were washed away when Christian Atsu converted a Yoan Gouffran cross following quick and accurate distribution from Darlow. Peerless.

UNITED: Darlow, Anita, Lascelles, Clark, Dummett, Ritchie (Atsu 69), Shelvey, Hayden, Gouffran, Diame, Gayle (Perez 82).

Unused: Sels, Lazaar, Mbemba, Yedlin, Mitrovic

Attendance: 14,562

Referee: Simon Hooper

Post-match league position: 1st

BURTON ALBION 1   NEWCASTLE UNITED 2

Pirelli Stadium

Saturday 17th December 2016

SCORERS:

Gayle	**15**	**1-0**
Dyer	20	1-1
Diame	**34**	**2-1**

Dwight Gayle had been lethal all season and suddenly Mo Diame was in a purple patch of his own with his third goal in his last five appearances as Newcastle won in their white and purple kit for the first time. At the home of The Brewers in the last game before Christmas it looked like everyone wanted to get things sorted out quickly with the goal-scoring wrapped up well before half time.

"Now we enjoy Christmas. Our fans will be happy and I wish everyone a Merry Christmas. I'm really pleased" smiled a beaming Benitez after another maximum return, this time from the tiny Pirelli Stadium, a ground whose capacity could fit into St. James' seven times with space to spare.

Credit to Burton though as they took the game to Newcastle having more shots, more possession and more corners. However it's goals that count and Newcastle's made to measure finishing was tailor made for a club managed by Clough, albeit Nigel.

Jonjo Shelvey ran the game. His vision opening up the home defence for the opening goal as he found Ritchie who in turn teed up Gayle who converted in front of an away following, unusually housed on a standing terrace.

Burton bounced back quickly, Lloyd Dyer getting on the end of a Jackson Irvine cross but Diame swept home the winner with only 34 minutes on the clock.

Top of the table and with a Boxing Day visit of Sheffield Wednesday to look forward to everything looked to be going well but there was still the prospect of losing key man Shelvey to a ban. Rafa had often alternated Jack Colback and Isaac Hayden alongside Shelvey but the Londoner was the man who so often made the team tick.

Three days after this victory at Burton came news that Shelvey had been found guilty of the charges against him stemming from the visit of Wolves three months earlier. A fine of £100,000 was meted out but potentially much more costly was the news that they player would be suspended for five games beginning with the Boxing Day visit of The Owls.

UNITED: Darlow, Yedlin, Lascelles, Clark, Dummett, Atsu, Shelvey, Hayden, Ritchie (Gouffran 85), Diame, Gayle.

Unused: Sels, Lazaar, Anita, Mbemba, Perez, Mitrovic

Attendance: 6,665

Referee: Lee Probert

Post-match league position: 1st

NEWCASTLE UNITED 0 SHEFFIELD WEDNESDAY 1

St. James'

Monday 26th December 2016

SCORERS:

Loovens   53   0-1

Having won four of their previous five games Wednesday came to Tyneside looking to establish themselves in a play-off place.

Both goalkeepers seemed determined to restrict any Christmas cheer by looking like they would keep the game goalless, until Dutch international defender Glenn Loovens broke the deadlock eight minutes into the second half with a header as Newcastle struggled to clear a corner. This brought about a fourth home defeat of the season, double the number of away reverses. At the other end Keiren Westwood was unbeatable on the day, albeit he needed the frame of the goal to help him withstand a Dwight Gayle shot he just managed to tip onto the post. That was the pick of the saves from the Republic of Ireland international who chalked up his 39th shut-out on his 101st appearance for the club.

Shelvey's absence took away much of the creativity from the home midfield and with Matt Ritchie missing much of the verve he'd displayed earlier in the campaign (with just one goal in his last nine appearances) Newcastle struggled to get out of third gear.

Wednesday's willingness to break quickly and in numbers when they won the ball was always a threat and Newcastle could never quite get on top of the game. Despite the disappointment the simple fact was that Newcastle were sitting pretty with the new year calendars about to be unveiled. New Year's Eve was to be looked forward to and before that the eagerly awaited re-match with Nottingham Forest.

UNITED: Darlow, Anita, Lascelles, Clark, Dummett, Ritchie, Hayden, Colback (Mitrovic 80), Gouffran (Atsu 62), Diame (Perez 69) Gayle.

Unused: Sels, Yedlin, Lazaar, Mbemba,

Attendance: 52,179

Referee: Paul Tierney

Post-match league position: 1st

NEWCASTLE UNITED 3 NOTTINGHAM FOREST 1

St. James'

Friday 30th December 2016

SCORERS:

Ritchie	**4**	**1-0**
Dimitru	29	1-1
Gayle	**63**	**2-1**
Gayle	**88**	**3-1**

Forest only had to play with 10 men rather than the nine Newcastle played with at their place but United took full advantage. The players were as eager as the fans to redress the balance having lost in such controversial circumstances at the City Ground just four weeks earlier and so it took just four minutes to take a very early lead. It was one of six times during the season that United raced out of the blocks with a goal in the first five minutes.

Despite defeat four days earlier the crowd against Forest increased from the traditional Boxing Day high to a best of the season, due at least in part to the wish to see Forest get their come-uppance. Just around the corner from St. James' the curtain was coming down on the last night of 'Beauty & the Beast' at the Tyne Theatre and Opera House. At St. James the man viewed by the fans as the beast hadn't turned up. Henri Lansbury however had not played since the earlier game with Newcastle and would move to Villa in January. He would appear at Newcastle in his sixth game for Villa when he would score an own goal and in time would help Villa deny Brighton on the last day of the season as Newcastle snatched the title – funny game football.

If Newcastle had no good fortune at Forest the fact that Matt Ritchie's deflected free kick left Vladimir Stojkovic wrong-footed was not something likely to elicit sympathy from anyone in black and white.

Forest trailed for 25 minutes before drawing level when Ciaran Clark couldn't cut out a Matthew Cash cross, enabling winger Nicolao Dimitru to head the equaliser with what would be his only goal in English football. On loan to Forest from Napoli, Dimitru had been on Napoli's books when Benitez was manager there but never played for Rafa as he was loaned out to Cittadella, Reggina and Veria during Rafa's reign.

The match had ticked around to the hour mark when it detonated. Forest's well-travelled Matt Mills wiped out Ayoze Perez for which he was rightly yellow carded. Unhappy with the decision the Forest skipper thrust the ball at Gayle rather too aggressively for the liking of the officials and to the delight of the crowd referee Mr. Stroud flourished a second yellow and with it a red.

United swiftly exacted revenge. Just three minutes later they went ahead when Gayle struck his 18th goal of the season to make it 2-1 before rubbing it in with another two minutes from time.

It was the first time the Gayle / Ritchie axis had both been on the mark in the same game since the 4-1 walloping of Reading in August. Significantly as 2016 ended a nine-point gap had been opened up over Reading in third place. That same nine-point cushion over Reading in third would still be there when it mattered most at the end of the season.

UNITED: Darlow, Yedlin, Lascelles, Clark, Dummett, Ritchie (Lazaar 83), Colback (Diame 67), Hayden, Atsu, Perez, Gayle (Mitrovic 88).

Unused: Sels, Mbemba, Anita, Gouffran.

Attendance: 52,228

Referee: Keith Stroud

Post-match league position: 1st

BLACKBURN ROVERS 1 NEWCASTLE UNITED 0

Ewood Park

Monday 2nd January 2017

SCORERS:

Mulgrew   74   0-1

This was very much a case of déjà vu for The Magpies who somehow managed to lose again to a team destined for relegation, astonishingly to a goal from the same player in almost exactly the same minute as he scored at St. James' earlier in the season.

It wasn't a good start to 2017 as Brighton took advantage of the slip to take over at the top of the table and yet there was a pre-match boost with the news that Mo Diame had been able to delay his departure to play in the African Cup of Nations for Senegal and indeed Diame was as good as anyone for Newcastle on the night.

Sometimes it's just not your day and this was one of them. A first half featuring 14 efforts on goal by United and none from Rovers illustrates the pattern of the game but ultimately it's not how much of the ball you have but what you do with it that matters, and it was the home side who succeeded in putting it in the back of the net.

When United did actually get the ball beyond former 'Boro goalie Jason Steele they twice had 'goals' disallowed.

Scotland international defender Charlie Mulgrew scored only three goals all season, but two of them were against Newcastle. Having scored the winner at St. James' he did so again here with a free kick, leaving Newcastle with just over quarter of an hour to get back into the match. Try as they might though there was simply no way through against a side who somehow kept two clean sheets against Newcastle, having only managed one other up to this point.

Both before and after the match home fans protested against their owners Venkys.

Rovers would return to the third tier they last played in in 1980, when they were promoted under Ryton born Howard Kendall. Rovers relegation at the end of the season made them the first Premier League champions to drop into the third level.

UNITED: Darlow, Anita (Murphy 87), Lascelles, Clark, Dummett, Ritchie, Hayden, Colback (Perez 77) Gouffran (Atsu 85), Diame, Gayle.

Unused: Sels, Lazaar, Mbemba, Yedlin.

Attendance: 18,524

Referee: Andy Woolmer

Post-match league position: 2nd

BIRMINGHAM CITY 1   NEWCASTLE UNITED 1

St. Andrew's

Saturday 7th January 2017

Emirates FA Cup 3rd round

SCORERS:

Murphy	**5**	**1-0**
Jutkiewicz	42	1-1

Buoyed by United's ambitions in the EFL Cup 4,671 journeyed to St. Andrews to see Newcastle take on a side well and truly hammered on Tyneside under a month earlier. However as is so often the case with cup ties in modern day football there were as many changes as there were thousands in the attendance: United making eight changes to Birmingham's five.

Encouragingly Massadio Haidara was back in action having been missing since October but that lift was soon cancelled out as Mitrovic was injured.

To the delight of many and the intrigue of all Benitez experimented with two up front in a 3-5-2 shape and saw Daryl Murphy score his first goal for the club after a mere five minutes. The former black cat pounced from close range to sweep home a badly defended corner in front of the Toon Army who licked their lips at the early advantage and the prospect of seeing how the team fared with a two-pronged attack.

This thought didn't have long to take hold though as the partnership was brought to a crushing end just five more minutes into the game when Mitrovic left on a stretcher apparently on oxygen. It was a worrying sight but the Serbian was back in action in the next round three weeks later, and while Gouffran came on to play in an advanced role the Murphy and Mitro due had looked like M for menace. "We had an idea with Mitrovic and Murphy but with Gouff it was different" explained the manager.

In a scrappy encounter Newcastle were unable to take the game away from Gianfranco Zola's outfit who were still looking for a first win under the Chelsea legend. Zola's side managed to equalise shortly before half time when former Middlesbrough pair Jonathan Grounds and Lukas Jutkiewicz combined for the latter to level from an unmarked position close to the centre of goal. Similarly slack marking twice allowed the striker clear views of Matz Sels' goal in the second half but his inability to direct his efforts on target meant a replay 11 days later.

UNITED: Sels, Yedlin, Lascelles, Hanley, Haidara, (Ritchie 70), Lazaar, Anita, Tiote (Hayden 65), Colback, Murphy, Mitrovic (Gouffran 10)

Unused: Darlow, Clark, Dummett, Gayle.

Attendance: 13,171

Referee: Neil Swarbrick

BRENTFORD 1   NEWCASTLE UNITED 2

Griffin Park

Saturday 14th January 2017

SCORERS:

Gayle	**20**	**1-0**
Vibe	52	1-1
Murphy	**79**	**2-1**

Dwight 'Goal' only had eight minutes to enjoy becoming the first man to score 20 goals in a season for Newcastle since Alan Shearer in 2003-04 before he had to depart due to a hamstring injury. It was a day when the three points were counter-balanced by as many injuries and Benitez even having to substitute a substitute.

"It was very difficult to get three points" reckoned Rafa who had the compensation of seeing Daryl Murphy come off the bench to register his first league goal for the club with a late winner, combined with seeing his side return to the top of the table courtesy of Preston North End beating Brighton.

Danish forward Lasse Vibe was the man who did his best to keep Brighton on top. He was a threat throughout, equalising early in the second half. Vibe also hit the post before the ball rolled agonisingly along the goal-line, as well as twice being denied by Darlow and once by a terrific block by Grant Hanley.

Brentford could count themselves unlucky not to earn a share of the spoils but United weren't complaining when Murphy materialised to head the winner 11 minutes from time.

UNITED: Darlow, Yedlin, Lascelles, Clark, Dummett, Ritchie, Hayden (Anita 62 / Hanley 72), Colback, Gouffran, Perez, Gayle (Murphy 28).

Unused: Sels, Lazaar, Ameobi, Sterry.

Attendance: 11,435

Referee: Chris Kavanagh

Post-match league position: 1st

NEWCASTLE UNITED 3 BIRMINGHAM CITY 1

St. James'

Wednesday 18th January 2017

Emirates FA Cup 3rd round replay

SCORERS:

Ritchie	9 pen	1-0
Gouffran	34	2-0
Cotterill	71	2-1
Ritchie	90+2	3-1

No one had wanted a replay as the focus was firmly on the home straight in the promotion race now that the season had passed the half way mark. Debuts for youngsters Stuart Findlay, Dan Barlaser and Yasin Ben El-Mhanni indicated that Rafa was already focussed on the weekend's league match, and that no chances were being taken even though it was against back markers Rotherham.

Scotland Under 21 international Findlay would not play again all season while El-Mhanni and Barlaser would make another appearance in the next round of the cup at Oxford. Celebrating his 20th birthday Barlaser had the chance to give himself the present of goal but couldn't convert the rebound when Ritchie hit the woodwork.

While seeing youngsters get a chance is always fascinating the most welcome sight on the team-sheet was the return of Jonjo Shelvey, now out of suspension and ready to rid himself of any rustiness.

An early Ritchie penalty duly added to by Gouffran's sixth goal of the season established cruise control against opposition limited by lack of confidence and the memory of their recent trip to the north east.

Only David Cotterill looked like he might register for the Blues, firing in a couple of shots from distance in the first half and with 19 minutes to go he halved the deficit to make everyone worry that the game might end up going to extra-time. The Wales international accepted a chance created by Maikel Kieftenbeld's header after Jutkiewicz's cleverly executed chip for a goal out of keeping with the rest of the visitors' performance.

Despite a few late worries however safe passage into the fourth round was secured deep into injury time when Ritchie's second goal of the night made him the fourth player of the season to register a brace, joining Gayle, Mitrovic and Perez, the latter who was making his 100th appearance for the club against Zola's team.

UNITED: Sels, Yedlin (Hayden 76), Hanley, Findlay, Lazaar, Ritchie, Tiote (Colback 83), Shelvey, El-Mhanni (Perez 70), Barlaser, Gouffran

Unused: Elliott, Dummett, Lascelles, Murphy

Attendance: 34,896

Referee: Lee Probert

NEWCASTLE UNITED 4 ROTHERHAM UNITED 0

St. James'

Saturday 21st January 2017

SCORERS:

Murphy	45+3	1-0
Ritchie	49	2-0
Perez	59	3-0
Ritchie	77	4-0

The miserable Millers would end up with fewer than quarter of the points the Magpies managed but put up strong resistance that was only broken deep into first half injury time by Daryl Murphy. Once ahead though the visitors were in cruise control with Matt Ritchie repeating his mid-week brace as four or more goals were scored for the sixth time with Ayoze Perez chipping in with the other goal.

Anthony Forde should have scored for the sky blue clad visitors after Darlow came rushing off his line without gathering cleanly. Perhaps that missed opportunity was playing on the minds of Paul Warne's side when they switched off seconds before the break. Caught out by Jonjo Shelvey who hit a magnificently accurate free kick from inside his own half to pick out the beacon that was blonde cropped DeAndre Yedlin. The USA international sped down the right before delivering a low cross. Killing it with his right foot, Murphy swivelled before curling an exquisite curling shot with his left from 12 yards. Murphy's first goal at St. James' was a Premier League quality strike out of keeping with the fare the first half had previously provided.

Resistance broken, Rotherham quickly crumbled. Only four minutes had been played after the half time pep-talks when Ritchie rifled in a rebound as Richard O'Donnell spilled a routine shot from Gouffran. Ten minutes later Yedlin reprieved his right flank running, getting round the back and pulling the ball back for Perez to further punish the South Yorkshire strugglers.

Full of confidence Newcastle looked like scoring every time they piled forward and completed the scoring when the dynamic duo of Shelvey and Ritchie linked up again. Carrying the ball over the half-way line Jonjo had options but released Ritchie whose low left foot shot went through a keeper playing his first game after joining the club from Bristol City two days earlier.

UNITED: Darlow, Yedlin (Sterry 80), Lascelles, Clark, Dummett, Ritchie, Hayden, Shelvey, Gouffran (Ameobi 64), Perez, Murphy (Lazaar 75)

Unused: Sels, Hanley, Haidara, Barlaser

Attendance: 52,208

Referee: Jeremy Simpson

Post-match league position: 1st

OXFORD UNITED 3   NEWCASTLE UNITED 0

Kassam Stadium

Saturday 28th January 2017

SCORERS:

Hemmings	46	0-1
Nelson	79	0-2
Martinez	87	0-3

Even though it had been a relatively comfortable stroll to easily beat Rotherham Rafa felt the need to make nine changes for this trip to League One Oxford United.

A minute's applause was held in tribute to the recently deceased U's stalwart Graham Atkinson but there was precious little requiring applause from a United point of view. A scrappy first half saw the Magpies scratch team struggle to find any fluency and perhaps Graham Atkinson's brother Big Ron was one of those yet to take their place for the second half when United fell behind inside a minute, as Kane

Hemmings scrambled a scruffy goal following a corner.

Newcastle's best chance of drawing level came almost half way through the second period only for 'keeper Simon Eastwood to save an Aleksandar Mitrovic penalty after the Serb had been fouled.

The introduction of Matt Ritchie 13 minutes from time raised hopes that Newcastle might find some spark. A replay wasn't wanted at the start but would have been welcomed as Ritchie entered the fray. Unfortunately, within a couple of minutes of Ritchie's entrance, any cup hopes were extinguished as Curtis Nelson headed home a corner with debutant Toni Martinez converting another late flag kick to make it 3-0 as this unfamiliar line-up continued to struggle with set-pieces.

After a decent run and unlucky exit in the League Cup to slip so meekly out of the FA Cup was a disappointment. However, the aim of the season was to win promotion. That was all that mattered. Benitez knows more about winning cups than anyone else at Newcastle and there would be time in the future to mount more serious challenges. The season was about to approach its closing stages and Newcastle's focus would be simple and straight-forward.

UNITED: Sels, Good, Hanley, Haidara (Ritchie 77), Gamez, Barlaser, Hayden, Lazaar, Perez, El-Mhanni (Gouffran 68), Mitrovic.

Unused: Elliott, Dummett, Shelvey, Yedlin

Attendance: 11,810

Referee: David Coote.

WINDOW SHOPPING

While Newcastle had been busy in the summer transfer market bringing a lot of new faces in and seeing some big names depart for colossal fees, January was a quiet month and evidently a disappointing one for the manager and fans. Hopes of boosting the squad for the second half of the season were dashed. Rumours abounded over the potential return of Andros Townsend from Crystal Palace but the only activity concerned a raft of loans for youngsters on the far fringes of the squad and the permanent departure of Cheick Tiote, who joined the rush to Chinese football with a transfer to Beijing Enterprises.

Goalkeeper Tim Krul ended one loan in the Netherlands with Ajax and began another with AZ while Sammy Ameobi returned from his loan to Bolton Wanderers for whom he had scored four times. Sammy would be given four Championship chances off the bench, although in total his playing time would be under an hour.

Reflecting on a transfer window which had left him without a real impact, Benitez was putting on a brave face in public but said to be smarting about it in private. "I'm disappointed but at the same time I have to concentrate on the players we have and try to improve them as much as we can" he said. "They can be very important players for this club. If we are promoted they will be famous..."

At least he would have players returning from the African Cup of Nations, a tournament Newcastle had lost Mohamed Diame, Christian Atsu and Chancel Mbemba to. Diame played just a single game in the tournament for Senegal. Atsu appeared half a dozen times for Ghana including the semi-final where they went down to Cameroon, while Mbemba played four times for DR Congo although he didn't play for United between November and April.

In March Mbemba would post a tweet saying, "Despite my minimal playing time this season, I am here and I am not giving up. I continue to train ardently and seriously and I will not give up until I find my place in the team. My wish is to come back stronger than ever and satisfy you, my fans, as I was able to do last season in the Premier League." Mbemba had apparently fallen out of favour with Benitez after the home defeat to Wolves in the autumn.

Benitez did not become one of the world's top managers without being a keen student of the game, a man who devises a specific game-plan to counteract the opposition's strengths. Mbemba hadn't stuck to the game-plan in terms of the areas he passed the ball into and had scored an own goal in a home defeat for good measure.

Since the Wolves debacle Chancel's only league appearance had been in the home defeat to Blackburn. He would eventually get his chance in April with four games followed by ending on a high with a goal as the title was clinched on the final day against Barnsley but for now it was more a case of Cancel Mbemba than Chancel Mbemba and United's squad for the run in was without the boost of a new face or two Benitez had hoped to install.

CHAPTER 10
FULL ON FOCUS

Consistency is the name of the game when it comes to winning any league title or promotion. In a championship campaign spread over 46 fixtures any decent side can hit a run of form where they look the business, but the teams who finish in the top two are the ones who over a whole season prove themselves to have been the most consistent.

The riches of the Promised Land of the Premier League are so vast that in the modern game there are many teams in the Championship who are prepared to gamble financially to mount a challenge for promotion. There are many former Premier League clubs who aspire to return and for every Rotherham happy to try and survive in the second tier there are a couple of clubs such as Wolves or Forest who have seen better times, have ambitions of reaching the top level again, but are still well short of the required standard as so many clubs scramble for the promotion places.

Amidst all this a club the size of Newcastle, with a squad of quantity as well as quality, had its own pressures. When Rafa and co walked through the doors of whichever ground they were visiting The Magpies were viewed as a scalp to be gained while a trip to St. James' usually didn't just provide the visitors with the biggest crowd they'd play in front of all year, often it was the biggest by upwards of 20,000 compared to their next highest. Sometimes such a stage could scare a side but perhaps even more often it could inspire them to raise their game, providing United with another obstacle to clear in their race to the top.

Having reached the summit Newcastle now had to deal with the slog of mid-season. The shortest month of February would bring seven fixtures as the relentless schedule continued. This is where Rafa's rotation earlier in the season would reap its rewards. At a time when other clubs were beginning to feel the strain, Benitez's players were fresher than they otherwise might have been. In several positions it was still hard to agree who was first choice so when a player came into the side he didn't feel second class or a fringe player joining the regulars. It was very much a squad game and everyone had a part to play.

Now that the January transfer window was over and the cup campaigns had ground to a halt, the squad was what it was. Rafa may have liked further strengthening but the undeniable truth was that Newcastle possessed the strongest squad in the league. The end of the season could be seen on the far horizon. United were in a strong position but by no means certain to go up. Brighton were only a point behind with a game in hand, and while Huddersfield, Leeds and Reading were at least three wins worth behind, things could change quickly - and there were still 57 points to play for. Would Newcastle blossom in the Spring and come up smelling of roses or would they become tangled in the undergrowth and end up on the compost heap?

NEWCASTLE UNITED 2 QPR 2

St. James'

Wednesday 1st February

SCORERS:

Shelvey	**1**	**1-0**
Washington	44	1-1
Ritchie	**54**	**2-1**
Clark O.G.	90	2-2

The visit of QPR perfectly encapsulated the pitfalls that lay in United's promotion path. Hammered 6-0 on their own patch, The Hoops were more awkward opposition at St. James' on a night which typified much of the season. As so often happened the visitors looked like rabbits caught in headlights as they fell behind to an early goal while they gaped at the size and sound of the audience, who had assembled to see them thrown to the slaughter. But as also often happened once they found their feet the opposition came back into the game and caught Newcastle's Achilles' Heel as they conceded just before the break. This was the sixth goal conceded in the five minutes before half time whereas only three other goals had been conceded in the opening 40 minutes! Scoring early in the second half was often a strong point following Benitez's words but unfortunately it also wasn't rare to leak a late goal and Newcastle would do all of these things against QPR who to the disappointment of many managed to take a point from Tyneside having been humiliated in West London.

Following on from the embarrassing cup defeat at Oxford so that the league could be concentrated on, the dropping of two points didn't go down well in the pubs and clubs. The cup exit was pondered in the light of this performance where only Hayden and Perez had started the cup-tie. Safe to say it didn't go down too well in the dressing room either.

The night had started brilliantly unless you were still on the way in after work and / or a pre-match pint. Shelvey wasn't waiting for late-comers as he opened the scoring with a delicious half-volley after just 37 seconds for his first goal since the reverse fixture. However, those hoping to settle back in their seats and enjoy watching the Londoners be systematically dismantled were to be let down. Maybe subconsciously this mind-set affected the players too. At least a routine win seemed set against a side who if they went two or three down might well collapse, leaving another six of the best score-line on the cards.

Rangers had replaced Jimmy Floyd Hasslebaink with Ian Holloway since the earlier meeting and refused to buckle, so as time moved on it became less of a game and more of a match. Chances started to come Rangers' way with Massimo Luongo twice missing the opportunity to make a name for himself on his return to the north-east, having played for Australia against England on Wearside at the end of the previous season. It came as no surprise when Rangers' equalised as Conor Washington nudged home his fifth goal of the season.

Shaken by their inability to establish control after their head start, and reminded of the need to ensure that crucial mid-season consistency, Newcastle re-emerged re-energised and came out on the front foot. This approach quickly paid off as Ritchie headed Toon back into the lead but try as they might the players could not create the cushion of a two goal advantage, leaving them open to the sort of late leveller they suffered at Aston Villa. Sure enough two points that would have taken Newcastle back to the top of the table were snatched away at the death when former Villa man Ciaran Clark couldn't avoid heading into his own goal as he strained to reach a cross from Newcastle old boy Kazenga LuaLua. Clark had scored at the right end in the corresponding fixture and it wasn't just him but the team who paid the price for not taking the chances as they had at Loftus Road. "We needed to score the third goal but we didn't do it" beseeched Benitez. Conceding late on matters less if games are already put to bed but dropping points like this again would give people nightmares.

UNITED: Darlow, Yedlin, Lascelles, Clark, Dummett, Ritchie, Shelvey, Hayden, Gouffran, Perez (Diame 86), Murphy (Ameobi 66).

Unused: Sels, Lazaar, Hanley, Gamez, Mitrovic

Attendance: 47,909

Referee: Tim Robinson

Post-match league position: 2nd

NEWCASTLE UNITED 1 DERBY COUNTY 0

St. James'

Saturday 4th February

SCORER:
Ritchie   27   1-0

Rumours of Rafa's unhappiness at the lack of transfer activity had grown so much throughout the week that even the return of Steve McClaren couldn't side-track the Toon Army who were determined to stand up to show they loved Rafa right from the kick off. The Rafa remainers had convinced Benitez to stick with the club in the championship and they were out in force to make sure that Rafa the Gaffer stayed in charge.

The sight of McClaren on the opposition bench only heightened the awareness of Bentez's importance to the club.

McClaren was simply the latest in a long line of managers with strong CV's, who hadn't been able to enhance those CV's in the cauldron of north east football. Benitez though was bringing back the heat to The Hotbed of Soccer, and if he was feeling the heat of a power- struggle behind the scenes the entire Toon Army were making it abundantly clear whose side they were on. Last off the pitch at the final whistle after saluting the fans, Rafa recognized that support which he understood was crucial not just to his own future but that of the success of the club.

The game itself was far from a classic but the stage of the season was being reached where points mattered much more than performances. United were worthy winners but had to work hard to edge the match.

On a day when the NUFC fans' Food Bank was launched, at times the forwards had to feed on scraps and take anything that came their way. Such was the way with the only goal of the game. Mid-way through the first half good approach play worked the ball to Matt Ritchie whose shot found the back of the net courtesy of a deflection off Bradley Johnson which left former England goalkeeper Scott Carson helpless.

Johnson's inadvertent deflection would not go down as an own goal unlike Ciaran Clark's in mid-week, but Clark had already shown his worth with a telling interception to deny Darren Bent. The former Sunderland and England striker would go even closer in injury time when DeAndre Yedlin was United's hero with a goal-line clearance.

Close shave though that was it wasn't the closest. Ten minutes from time with the goal at his mercy Tom Ince thankfully fired wide. It was a let-off but one accepted as gratefully as the people benefiting from the Food Bank.

"In the second half we were fantastic and should not have lost that game" claimed Steve McClaren back at St. James's as Derby boss 11 months after being sacked. Such assessment seemed more than familiar as the ex-England manager sought to explain how somehow despite being fantastic his side had failed to score and lost. At Newcastle he failed to win 22 of his 28 Premier League games but now those days were gone and under Benitez United eked out exactly the kind of mid-season result that wins leagues. It wasn't a good performance and it wasn't an exciting one but when the Sunday papers came out there were three more points added to Newcastle's tally and ultimately this was all that mattered.

UNITED: Darlow, Yedlin, Hanley, Clark, Dummett, Ritchie, Shelvey, Hayden (Perez 49), Gouffran (Lascelles 90+2), Diame, Mitrovic (Ameobi 84).

Unused: Elliott, Lazaar, Gamez, Murphy.

Attendance: 52,271

Referee: Darren Bond.

Post-match league position: 1st

WOLVERHAMPTON WANDERERS 0 NEWCASTLE UNITED 1

Molineux

Saturday 11th February

SCORER:
Mitrovic   44   1-0

Aleksandar Mitrovic had missed too many chances against Derby in midweek but rammed home the winner here. Back to back 1-0 wins were exactly what was required if that mid-season consistency was to be achieved. Efficiency was the key and single goal wins complete with clean sheets kept the points total on the move, and would deflate the chasing pack every time United's result was confirmed. Just as Chelsea burned off Spurs in the Premier League despite the latter's nine game winning run, having got in front Newcastle had to maintain the gap and increase it if they could.

While Brighton were hot on the leader's heels, still just a point behind, the most important gap beyond the top two had stretched to a healthy seven points to third placed Huddersfield. With United's goal difference by now a magnificent 35 (from 30 games) compared to The Terriers plus six, effectively that seven-point gap was as good as eight. A further point behind Huddersfield fourth placed Reading had also played a game more, as had Leeds who were 11 points behind Newcastle. In the final play off place on the same games as The Magpies Sheffield Wednesday were fully 13 points behind United.

Of the clubs relegated alongside Newcastle, Norwich still harboured hopes of an instant return although they had work to do being two points behind The Owls despite playing a game more. Aston Villa though had concerns at the other end of the table. Looking over their shoulder they were only seven points clear of the drop but 16 away from the Play offs and a massive 29 behind Newcastle. This only further served to show what a good job Benitez was doing because Villa had invested in their squad too but were struggling to adapt.

You need a bit of luck to win anything and United appeared to have some at Molineux where Mitrovic might have been sent off before he had the chance to notch the game's only goal. Already in the book the Serb was spared a second yellow after a robust challenge on 'keeper Carl Ikeme. Having scored a minute before half time, Mitrovic didn't emerge for the second half, Benitez evidently electing to not run the risk of his striker being red carded. That was simply good management as Rafa led by example when it came to consistency by always making decisions based on what he felt was right for the team. "I think it was important to protect him and protect the team" Rafa explained later, adding, "I wanted to be sure that we had 11 players on the pitch."

UNITED: Darlow, Yedlin, Lascelles, Clark, Dummett, Ritchie (Murphy 82), Colback, Shelvey, Gouffran, Diame (Perez 82), Mitrovic (Atsu 46).

Unused: Elliott, Hanley, Gamez, Hayden.

Attendance: 24,876

Referee: Craig Pawson

Post-match league position: 1st

NORWICH CITY 2   NEWCASTLE UNITED 2

Carrow Road

Tuesday 14th February

SCORERS:

Perez	**1**	**1-0**
Murphy	12	1-1
Jerome	17	1-2
Lascelles	**81**	**2-2**

If Newcastle had an extra motive to beat Nottingham Forest when they got them on their own patch then The Canaries were almost as eager to redress the balance against Newcastle. It wasn't that Alex Neil's side felt as cheated as Newcastle fans had at Forest, but having been top of the table when leading deep into injury team before losing and subsequently slipping out of the leading pack, they were determined to put things right.

That determination came to the fore when they took the lead after little over quarter of an hour as they responded to falling behind after little over quarter of a minute! Restored to the starting line-up Ayoze Perez struck after a mere 23 seconds as Newcastle continued to come out of the blocks quicker than Usain Bolt. This was United's third first minute goal of the season, and the quickest.

Undaunted, the home side drew level in the 12th minute with one of the best goals scored against Newcastle all season. The move began with 'keeper John Ruddy and concluded with Jacob Murphy (whose twin brother Josh later came on as sub) neatly finishing from close range. Five minutes later United fell behind. Cameron Jerome had provided the assist for the equaliser and quickly added his own name to the score-sheet when a rare mistake from Karl Darlow provided a Valentine's Day gift for the Huddersfield born player. As with Norwich's first goal the move began with a 'keeper – only this time it was Newcastle's as Darlow's poor clearance left Jerome to gleefully accept the easiest of chances to take his own goals tally for the season so far into double figures.

With over three-quarters of the game to go Newcastle had ample time to rescue the match but they had to wait before adding to Perez's very early goal. It was starting to look as if it wasn't to be United's night as Ritchie hit the underside of the bar and chances came and went. Norwich had led for over an hour when their defence was broken as Perez matched Jerome in claiming an assist as well as a goal. Ayoze's cross arrowed to Jamaal Lascelles who equalised with nine minutes to go to make it a happier overnight drive home for the Toon Army, many of whom had some explaining to do about why they'd travelled to see the match instead of taking their other half out.

UNITED: Darlow, Yedlin, Lascelles, Clark, Dummett, Ritchie (Atsu 70), Shelvey, Colback (Diame 54), Gouffran, Perez 82, Mitrovic (Gayle 76).

Unused: Elliott, Hanley, Gamez, Hayden.

Attendance: 26,841

Referee: Andy Madley

Post-match league position: 1st

NEWCASTLE UNITED 2 ASTON VILLA 0

St. James'

Monday 21st February

SCORERS:

Gouffran	42	1-0
Lansbury O.G.	59	2-0

Having failed to show for Forest in their return fixture at St. James', following his move to Aston Villa Henri Lansbury was in midfield for the visitors but probably wished he wasn't. Hounded by The Toon Army for his part in the Forest fiasco two and a half months earlier Lansbury

Newcastle United
manager Rafa Benitez.

13/09/16: Jonjo Shelvey celebrates his goal at QPR. It was the most spectacular of the six scored on a sensational night.

28/09/16: Dwight's delirium! Gayle blows Norwich away with the winner in the dramatic 4-3 victory over the Canaries.

20/11/16: Gayle scores away to Leeds.

02/12/16: Both red cards received at Forest were later rescinded, including this one for Paul Dummett.

10/12/16: Gayle grabbed a second hat-trick of the season against Birmingham.

20/02/17: Everyone's favourite former Forest player Henri Lansbury scores an own goal when playing for Villa.

25/02/17: Player of the Year Ciaran Clark scores against Bristol City.

28/02/17: Perez plunders one of the most important goals of the season, at Brighton.

04/03/17 Daryl Murphy and Matt Ritchie celebrate in the win at Huddersfield.

01/04/17: One of the success stories of the season, Matt Ritchie celebrates against Wigan.

24/04/17: Christian Atsu, Ayoze Perez and DeAndre Yedlin are all smiles as promotion is confirmed against Preston.

24/04/17: Rafa thanks the fans but the thanks were all due to him.

07/05/17: Jack Grealish scores for Villa v Brighton to secure the title for Newcastle.

07/05/17: That Championship feeling!

07/05/17: Champagne moment.

07/05/17: Rafa Benitez is no stranger to silverware and thanks to him neither are the Toon!

scored an own goal even described as comical by Villa boss Steve Bruce.

This was a pedestrian match which never got into the higher gears. Both goals were scrambled efforts from corners but the important thing once again was that another victory was chalked up and the march back to the top-flight maintained momentum.

Villa had looked better than a team with just one point since the turn of the year before Newcastle nudged ahead after 42 minutes. Ritchie worked a short corner with Shelvey before whipping in a cross that saw both centre-backs Lascelles and Clark each try to knock the ball into the danger area before being partly blocked by Mile Jedinak. Villa didn't succeed in clearing their lines though, leaving Yoan Gouffran to squeeze home the all-important first goal from close range.

The second goal was just as scrappy but will live longer in the memory. Having been sent off at Forest for tangling with Lansbury, Shelvey delivered the flag-kick which was headed on by Jamaal Lascelles. His own goal back at his old club Forest had provided the skipper with his own horrors but on this occasion the nightmare was Lansbury's. Not concentrating and half holding onto the post he was meant to be guarding the ex-Arsenal player made a dog's breakfast of what should have been a simple clearance, instead scoring an own goal that delighted the home fans maybe even more than a Shelvey special might have.

Villa would do Newcastle a massive favour on the final day of the season with a late equaliser against Brighton that handed United the championship trophy, but for now three points was all that was asked.

UNITED: Darlow, Yedlin, Lascelles, Clark, Dummett, Ritchie, Shelvey, Colback, Diame, Gouffran (Atsu 88), Gayle (Mitrovic 33).

Unused: Elliott, Hanley, Lazaar, Gamez, Perez.

Attendance: 50,024

Referee: Peter Bankes

Post-match league position: 1st

NEWCASTLE UNITED 2   BRISTOL CITY 2

St. James'

Saturday 25th February

SCORERS:

Wilbraham	11	0-1
Cotterill	21	0-2
Smith O.G.	**59**	**1-2**
Clark	**82**	**2-2**

It's always best to win of course but if you can't win don't lose. Such an attitude is what cements unbeaten runs and it is unbeaten runs that maintain confidence and provide consistency. So even when a team has an off day if they can come away unbeaten that has to be seen as a positive, because not even the best teams can win every time.

Maybe there was a little bit of over-confidence going into this match even though recent displays had lacked the sort of fluency and clinical finishing which had marked more exciting stages of the season. Hovering just above the relegation zone Bristol City had lost 10 of their previous 13 games while Newcastle were unbeaten in six.

Fifth in mid-October after a bright start, The Robins had been awkward opponents as Newcastle had won narrowly at Ashton Gate back in the first month of the season. In contrast they looked like potential lambs to the slaughter as they took to the field at Newcastle. The only victories in their previous 16 matches had been 1-0 wins over rock bottom Rotherham and a cup replay success over League One Fleetwood.

Turning the form book on its head, Bristol became one of those sides inspired by the scale of the occasion at St. James'. Not only did they find themselves 2-0 to the good after just over 20 minutes, they were still commanding that two goal advantage with barely half an hour left.

Other than a couple of penalties the only goals Wales international forward David Cotterill scored all season were at St. James'. He'd netted in an FA Cup replay for Birmingham just over a month earlier and repeated the trick by tapping into an open goal when Paul Dummett's attempted header back to Karl Darlow only succeeded in causing calamity.

City couldn't believe their luck. They were already a goal to the good thanks to veteran Aaron Wilbraham heading them in front 10 minutes earlier. Newcastle had come back from a two goal deficit before and had plenty of time to do so again. The crowd and both sides knew this. The visitors also understood that once United got one and turned the sound up it would be even harder for them to protect their lead.

United patiently probed but it took an own goal to get them back into the game with half an hour to go to search for an equaliser and ideally a winner. Jonjo Shelvey was in the thick of it as he met a cross from Christian Atsu with City defender Korey Smith's desperate attempt to block only succeeding in taking it beyond his 'keeper Gabian Geifer.

City then kept United at bay for longer than it had taken them to establish their two goal lead but there were still eight minutes on the clock when Ciaran Clark headed home a Ritchie corner to tie up the game at 2-2.

Try as they might Newcastle just couldn't find a winner to mark Benitez's 50th game in charge but more worryingly this home draw meant four points had been dropped from the last nine on offer with two of those games requiring late equalisers to earn a point. This was a bad time for a blip as the next three games were away to the three nearest challengers.

UNITED: Darlow, Yedlin, Lascelles, Clark, Dummett, Shelvey, Colback (Diame 58), Ritchie, Perez (Gouffran 79) Atsu, Mitrovic.

Unused: Elliott, Hanley, Gamez, Anita, Murphy.

Att: 52,131

Referee: Chris Kavanagh

Post-match league position: 2nd

BRIGHTON AND HOVE ALBION 1   NEWCASTLE UNITED 2

The Amex Stadium

Tuesday 28th February

SCORERS:

Murray	14p	0-1
Diame	**81**	**1-1**
Perez	**89**	**2-1**

To Chris Hughton's credit Brighton were the team who managed to keep pace with Newcastle and prevent the promotion season being simply a stroll to the title. Albion's ability to keep alternating pole position with United kept stimulating Newcastle to greater heights. All the while this battle between the top two was going on the chasing pack were exactly that – chasing. Reading and Huddersfield particularly sometimes succeeded in narrowing the gap to a few points, but Newcastle were never out of the top two after beating Barnsley in mid-October, while Brighton were never out of the automatic positions after walloping Norwich 5-0 11 days later.

Going into this showdown Brighton were full of confidence. Three days earlier they had handsomely seen off Reading by 3-0 and started the game a point ahead, with the opportunity to open up a four-point gap if they could win.

When an early penalty converted by Glenn Murray put them in front, United faced probably their biggest challenge since the late, late come-back at home to Norwich. They had been under the cosh early on when Benitez would have been pleased he'd kept faith in Karl Darlow after a couple of costly recent errors as the 'keeper made a couple of early saves even before Murray's penalty got The Seagulls off to a flier.

Gradually Rafa's side started to come into the game, Ritchie and Atsu having first half efforts that reminded the home team they too had a fight on their hands. As the game opened up a little, with Newcastle needing an equaliser and Brighton looking to strengthen their advantage, it was evident that the next goal would be crucial. Another for Brighton would give Newcastle a much steeper mountain to climb than those they'd overcome when two goals down to more lowly opposition, while an equaliser for the visitors would test the home side's nerves and ability to handle the big occasion.

That key goal might have gone Brighton's way but for Paul Dummett's brilliant covering as he managed to clear off the line from Lewis Dunk early in the second half, but as the half wore on it was David Stockdale who became the busier goalkeeper.

Holding midfielder Jack Colback was removed to make way for attacker Daryl Murphy with just over quarter of an hour to go, with Murphy soon testing Stockdale as Newcastle upped the ante.

While United didn't make a change until the closing stages, the home side had been forced to replace WBA loannee Sebastien Pocognoli early on with Chelsea loannee Fikayo Tomori. He had a tough game through-out against his Chelsea club-mate Christian Atsu. It was Atsu who would turn the game and ultimately a result that would help Newcastle pip Brighton to the title.

Rafa was renowned for a come-back or two even before coming to Newcastle where in particular the turnaround against Norwich had sparked a comparison with a certain night in Istanbul during Benitez's Liverpool days. Here at Brighton the match may have been Championship rather than Champions League but it was still a very important game and one where once again Rafa found the key to keeping control and finding a solution.

Just as the home fans were sensing the final whistle wasn't too far away Newcastle's persistence paid off. The equaliser, when it came, carried a bit of good fortune but there had been plenty of misfortune on the night too, not least a debateable penalty award for the opening goal. Picking up possession on the edge of the box Atsu let fly, his shot deflecting off Daryl Murphy and Mo Diame – the latter being credited with the goal- as Stockdale was finally beaten.

With Newcastle now with their tails up and Brighton deflated Benitez decided to twist rather than stick, bringing on Ayoze Perez for Yoan Gouffran. With barely a minute on the clock Ritchie found Atsu with a pass almost as long as Brighton Pier and from the Chelsea man's cross who else but Perez was there to finish from close range and cue delirium in the 2,900 in the away end, for whom the 692 mile round trip on a school night suddenly seemed as short a hop as a trip to Whitley Bay.

Brighton's five and a half month long unbeaten home record had been smashed as Newcastle leap-frogged them to lead the table by two points. Moreover the visit of Newcastle Brighton had been waiting for had been and gone without them being able to take advantage. Undoubtedly United were now the team in the driving seat as the finishing line of the season started to come into view.

UNITED: Darlow, Yedlin, Lascelles, Clark, Dummett, Atsu, Shelvey, Colback (Murphy 74), Ritchie, Diame, Gouffran (Perez 82).

Unused: Elliott, Hanley, Gamez, Anita, Mitrovic

Attendance: 30,230

Referee: Robert Madley

Post-match league position: 1st

CHRISTIAN ATSU

Signed on a season long loan from Chelsea, wide man Christian Atsu enjoyed one of his best games of the season in the key game at Brighton. Frequently used off the bench, 17 of his 32 Championship appearances were as a sub while in only eight of his 15 league starts did he last the distance.

Like a lot of wingers, when it came to consistency, Christian could blow hot and cold. Sometimes his crossing and final ball could frustrate while when he got it right the Ghana international could be devastating.

United had until the middle of May to decide whether to trigger a £6.5m release clause with over 80% of readers in a local newspaper poll wanting to sign him.

HUDDERSFIELD TOWN 1   NEWCASTLE UNITED 3

John Smith's Stadium

Saturday 4th March

SCORERS:

Ritchie	**10p**	**1-0**
Murphy	**32**	**2-0**
Mooy	72p	2-1
Gayle	**90**	**3-1**

The week long viewed as pivotal was proving hugely successful. Seemingly dismayed by losing late on to Newcastle in midweek Brighton lost another two late goals at Nottingham Forest where they were trounced 3-0 before The Toon kicked off. This left Newcastle with the opportunity to open up a five-point gap if they could also win at Huddersfield which is exactly what they did.

Not only did this handsome victory open up a comfortable gap with Brighton it stretched the lead over third placed Huddersfield to 11 points with as many games to go. It was looking good, albeit Huddersfield also had a game in hand.

Having fallen behind to an early spot kick at Brighton, United went ahead with an early one at Huddersfield when Ritchie was brought down by a forward's challenge by Nakhi Wells; the scorer of the first goal seen at St. James' this season. Ritchie picked himself up to despatch the penalty with aplomb and give Newcastle the upper hand in front of a record league crowd at the John Smith's Stadium.

David Wagner's surprise package gave as good as they got but lacked Newcastle's cutting edge, a fact highlighted when Daryl Murphy; making his first away league start, extended the lead just past the half hour mark.

Having got the goals United were reasonably content to let Huddersfield have the ball. A staggering stat of Newcastle having possession for under a quarter of the match illustrates that the Yorkshire side had a lot of the game but until they pulled a goal back with 18 minutes to go United were comfortable.

The boot had been on the other foot a few nights earlier at Brighton when it had been Newcastle's turn to respond from going behind early on before finally earning a breakthrough in the latter stages. Thankfully United had the cushion of a two goal lead and so retained control even after Aaron Mooy halved the lead with the game's second penalty, given for a Shelvey foul on Elias Kachunga.

With their tails up, The Terriers tore at the visitors who not only stood firm but capped a fabulous week by scoring on the break after Town's sub 'keeper Joel Coleman was stranded after coming up for a late corner. What made it even better was the goal came from leading marksman Dwight Gayle, back in action off the bench following injury. It was Gayle's first goal since January and his return could only further boost high-flying Newcastle, who with this victory equalled the club record of 13 league away wins in a season.

UNITED: Darlow, Anita, Lascelles, Clark, Dummett, Atsu (Yedlin 81), Shelvey, Colback (Gouffran 72), Ritchie, Diame, Murphy (Gayle 66).

Unused: Elliott, Hanley, Gamez, Perez.

Attendance: 23,213

Referee: Roger East

Post-match league position: 1st

READING 0 NEWCASTLE UNITED 0

Madjeski Stadium

Tuesday 7th March

Taking three points from The Madjeski Stadium would have been greedy. A winner at heart, Rafa was greedy, "Our fans travelling away will be happy with these seven points but it still could've been more" insisted Benitez. Nonetheless, collecting a magnificent seventh point from the last of the trio of away fixtures at the homes of Newcastle's closest rivals was an outstanding achievement. Significantly the point Reading gained from United's first goalless draw of the campaign represented the solitary point gleaned by United's opponents during this run, as they all missed the chance to maximise home advantage against the league leaders.

As at Huddersfield Newcastle saw precious little of the ball, this time 30% although as Leicester proved beyond doubt the season before, it's not how much of the ball you have that matters, it's what you do with it.

Jaap Stam's side boasted the best home record in the Championship and had won all but two of their last 11 home games so were eager to test themselves against United.

Both sides hit the frame of the goal, Ritchie rattling the post from the edge of the box while Garath McCleary hit the bar. However despite Reading's possession United's defence were so resolute that Darlow was only seriously tested once, thwarting Yann Kermorgant's volley.

UNITED: Darlow, Gamez, Lascelles, Clark, Dummett, Ritchie, Shelvey, Colback (Diame 88), Gouffran (Atsu 69), Perez, Murphy (Gayle 75).

Unused: Elliott, Hanley, Anita, Mbemba.

Attendance: 23,121

Referee: Andy Davies

Post-match league position: 1st

STILL WORK TO BE DONE

Since the cup exit at Oxford, Newcastle had played nine times, winning five and drawing four, remaining unbeaten despite trips to three of their closest challengers and averaging over two points a game since going out of the cup. It was now 11 league games without defeat since the turn of the year slip up against Blackburn, but there was still work to be done in the final ten fixtures.

Brighton were still hot on United's heels, just three points behind while Huddersfield had moved up to third and if they won their game in hand would be just six points adrift. Reading, Leeds and the rest now had too much ground to make up barring a sensational fall from grace by The Magpies but nothing could be taken for granted. Back to back defeats and almost a season's worth of hard work could be wiped out.

Chapter 11
RAFA'S RUN IN

The season had started against Fulham and the return visit of The Cottagers would mark the first anniversary of Rafa taking over as well as signalling the countdown to the end of the campaign, as United commenced their final 10 games spread over 58 days. Despite the false start that had seen them lose the opening two matches way back in August Newcastle were in a strong position to gain automatic promotion. This was the clear aim because no-one wanted to be involved in the Play Offs, that was the target of the men from Craven Cottage.

NEWCASTLE UNITED 1   FULHAM 3

St. James'

Saturday 11th March

SCORERS:

Cairney	15	0-1
Sessegnon	51	0-2
Sessegnon	59	0-3
Murphy	**76**	**1-3**

Fulham arrived on Tyneside filled with confidence. Unbeaten in half a dozen league games, Slavisa Jokanovic's side had been steadily reeling in the Play-off pack as they recovered from an Autumn wobble which had seen them drift into mid-table after a bright start.

In 16 year-old Ryan Sessegnon the visitors had one of the stand out names in the Championship and he would certainly make a name for himself at St. James'

Newcastle needed goal difference to keep them on top of the table after this defeat combined with Brighton's Friday night win over Derby.

The two leading sides were tied on 77 points as Huddersfield closed in, having the possibility of narrowing the gap to three points if they won their game in hand.

Back on home soil after a triumphal trio of away trips United were again out of sorts in front of their home fans. Just as in the previous home game when they'd had to come from two down to rescue a point against Bristol City, once more The Toon Army saw their team torn apart by the visitors, for whom their 16 year old full back scored twice and won a penalty Fulham could afford to miss.

As in recent games Newcastle couldn't get the ball but this time seeing the other team have the bulk of possession (62%) was in front of a home crowd increasingly frustrated as they expected their top of the table team to deliver.

Things certainly weren't helped when captain Tom Cairney hit a 'worldy' to put Newcastle a goal down after quarter of an hour. Despite Dwight Gayle's first start since limping out of the first half against Villa almost three weeks earlier Newcastle just couldn't get going.

Hopes of an improvement after half time quickly collapsed as Sessegnon scored twice to effectively end the contest against a lethargic home side before an hour was played. The youngster could easily have had a hat-trick after winning an injury time penalty. He wanted to take it only for USA international Tim Ream to spare United further disappointment by hitting the post with the spot-kick.

Although Daryl Murphy pulled a well-taken goal back, a fight-back never seemed on as Fulham maintained control. The sight of such an in-form team playing fluently and heading towards the play-offs with momentum served to emphasise how vital it was that Newcastle finished the job in the run-in by ensuring they finished in the top two. Running the risk of having an off day such as this in the Play offs against confident and cohesive opponents didn't bear thinking about.

UNITED: Darlow, Anita, Lascelles, Clark (Gamez 64), Dummett, Atsu, Colback, Shelvey, Ritchie, Diame (Murphy 61), Gayle (Gouffran 74)

Unused: Elliott, Hanley, Perez. Mitrovic

Attendance: 51,903

Referee: James Linington

Post-match league position: 1st

BIRMINGHAM CITY 0   NEWCASTLE UNITED 0

St. Andrew's

Saturday 18th March

A fourth meeting of the season with The Blues produced just the second goalless draw United had been involved in in 45 league and cup games, but the second in three matches. It was the first time in nine years that back to back away goalless draws had been recorded. Having got used to winning away in a record breaking season a point was something of a let-down at a club who had lost their last three home games, including one to doomed Wigan Athletic last time out at St. Andrew's.

Of course Newcastle had already drawn once on this ground in the cup and the point gained looked better when Brighton lost to Leeds in a late kick-off, leaving Newcastle in a better position than at the start of the day. Always one to look at the big picture, prior to the Brighton result Rafa remarked, "People may expect us to win every game but this was a valuable away point." With Huddersfield having lost heavily at Bristol City the evening before that was certainly the case. One point might have been less than the target from this fixture but it was a point more than either of the closest rivals gained that weekend and so a better outcome than had all three won. Going into an international break United had edged a tiny bit further in front as the games began to run out.

Given that only nine goals had been conceded in the 13 games he'd appeared in – and three of them in the cup at Oxford – former Blackburn centre back Grant Hanley could consider himself unfortunate not to have played more and here he got only his second league start since the start of the season. He performed admirably in helping towards a clean sheet, as he had on his previous appearance in the narrow win over Derby.

A relatively uneventful 90 minutes saw the biggest talking point being the disallowing of what looked like a late winner from Matt Ritchie in front of the Toon Army, Ritchie being ruled offside.

UNITED: Darlow, Anita, Lascelles, Hanley, Dummett, Ritchie, Diame, Colback, Gouffran (Atsu 82), Perez (Shelvey 78). Murphy (Gayle 63)

Unused: Elliott, Gamez, Mbemba, Mitrovic.

Attendance: 19,796

Referee: Simon Hooper

Post-match league position: 1st

NEWCASTLE UNITED 2 WIGAN ATHLETIC 1

St. James'

Saturday 1st April

SCORERS

Gayle	**36**	**1-0**
Jacobs	50	1-1
Ritchie	**57**	**2-1**

A first win in four games was hard won against opponents battling against the drop and lifted by it being interim manager Graham Barrow's first game in charge. However the points were won, all that mattered at this stage of the season was the result. Come 2017-18 when the likes of Chelsea, Liverpool and the Manchester clubs were on the fixture list no-one would be remotely bothered about how United had got back into the Premier League, just that they had achieved it.

United were the better side but Wigan coped well early on before Mo Diame set up Dwight Gayle to open the scoring at the far post nine minutes before the break. Spiritedly Wigan drew level early in the second half with Michael Jacobs turned in Alex Gilbey's delivery.

Latics were level for just a few minutes though as Newcastle's lead was quickly restored when an alert Matt Ritchie was first to react when his own half-volley came back off the woodwork, Ritchie heading home what proved to be the winner although he passed up the chance to extend the lead when put through by Atsu only for 'keeper Matt Gilks to block when Ritchie seemed a certain scorer, while the Scot was also denied what looked a stonewall penalty when brought down late on by Jake Buxton.

As a spectacle the match had been mundane but fans could enjoy looking at the league table because although Brighton had won, Huddersfield had lost. Consequently a massive 10 point cushion had opened up with only seven games to play, albeit Huddersfield still had a game in hand.

Ever practical, Rafa admitted, "I would like to score five goals and be amazing, but at the moment we showed character, good reaction and personality to manage the situation." The situation was looking good and promotion was undoubtedly now Newcastle's to lose rather than win. The question was would they freeze or continue to have the personality to manage the situation?

UNITED: Darlow, Anita, Lascelles, Hanley, Dummett, Ritchie, Shelvey, Colback, Gouffran (Hayden 70), Diame (Atsu 63), Gayle (Perez 80)

Unused: Elliott, Gamez, Mbemba, Mitrovic.

Attendance: 51,849

Referee: David Coote

Post-match league position: 1st

NEWCASTLE UNITED 1 BURTON ALBION 0

St. James'

Wednesday 5th April

SCORER:

Ritchie   68   1-0

Beating lowly Burton and Wigan within a few days was all that mattered. The days of 6-0 score-lines over QPR and Preston had gone for the moment, but much more importantly the simple fact was United had extrapolated a maximum six points out of these fixtures.

Burton had beaten Huddersfield on their own patch the previous weekend with a winner six minutes into added time so had to be taken seriously. Granted they are a small club but so were Wimbledon when they managed to win the FA Cup. Burton were in the championship on merit and commanded Rafa's respect even if some felt Newcastle should wipe the floor with them.

Penalties are simple things. Awarding penalties can be exceptionally difficult to get right, especially in an age when players dive in the box as soon as someone looks at them. Once a spot-kick is awarded though, administering its procedure is simple. Unlike in open play it is easy to see what is going on and the match officials themselves are static, not trying to make key decisions while running.

At Manchester City on May 13th Bobby Madley correctly gave a free kick to the home side when Leicester's Riyad Mahrez thought he'd scored from the spot. TV replays showed the eagle-eyed ref and noticed Mahrez had slipped in taking the penalty, inadvertently kicking the ball with both feet. The referee correctly disallowed the goal and penalised the penalty taker for taking two touches.

There was no such clear understanding of the Laws of the game by the officials for the Burton match at St. James'.

With just under half an hour played Newcastle were awarded a penalty which was converted by Matt Ritchie. However referee Keith Stroud spotted Dwight Gayle encroaching and penalised him. Nothing wrong with that...except the punishment should have been that the penalty would have to be re-taken. Amazingly, instead Mr. Stroud awarded a free kick to Burton!

Referees have the hardest job in football. Making decisions at break-neck speed while running yourself it is impossible to get every single one right. Football is a passionate game and top level football can have millions of pounds hinging on key decisions. Managers, pundits and fans can have several TV replays to see exactly what actually happened in key incidents and will usually then berate officials if they got a call incorrect from one viewing in real time.

On this occasion though a referee deemed good enough to officiate in the Championship before over 50,000 people simply did not know the Laws of the game. Moreover none of his assistant referees including the fourth official were clued up or confident enough to correct him.

Soon after the match the referees' organisation the Professional Game Match Officials Limited issued a statement explaining, "In this evening's EFL Championship game between Newcastle United and Burton Albion, referee Keith Stroud awarded Newcastle a penalty in the 29th minute. As Matt Ritchie took the kick, Dwight Gayle encroached in the penalty area. An indirect free-kick was awarded to Burton, but the Laws of the Game state that the penalty kick should have been re-taken. Unfortunately the referee has misapplied the Law."

All this of course was of no consolation to Newcastle and it is just as well that United went on to win the game, Ritchie himself getting the winner.

Instead of being a goal up in the first half and therefore Burton having to come out and play a bit more, the penalty reprieve gave the visitors licence to sit back with a 'what we have we hold' mentality.

Nigel Clough's Brewers did indeed hang on to a point until three quarters of the way through the match when Matt Ritchie spectacularly curled in what proved to be the winner.

Amidst the furore of what was one of the talking points of the season, not just this game it was easy to overlook the fact that the result guaranteed Newcastle the minimum of a top six place and that it was the first time since 2013 that back to back home league wins had been recorded.

Maximum points returns were what mattered most. While Brighton had won the night before, news came through that Huddersfield had lost at Norwich. Even if the Terriers were to win their game in hand they would have to claw back seven points and a vastly inferior goal difference and would only have six games to do it. The ultimate target was rapidly drawing closer.

UNITED: Darlow, Anita, Lascelles, Mbemba, Dummett, Ritchie, Shelvey, Diame, Atsu (Ameobi 89), Perez, Gayle (Murphy 90+1)

Unused: Elliott, Gamez, Hanley, Gouffran, Mitrovic.

Attendance: 48,814

Referee: Keith Stroud

Post-match league position: 1st

SHEFFIELD WEDNESDAY 2 NEWCASTLE UNITED 1

Hillsborough

Saturday 8th April

SCORERS:

Lees	59	0-1
Fletcher	68	0-2
Shelvey	**88**	**1-2**

Newcastle still weren't themselves. Having edged narrow home wins against struggling sides following two goalless draws and a home defeat from the previous three games, United hadn't fired on all cylinders for a while. As with the last time they encountered a Play-off contender

(Fulham) they were second best and had no complaints about leaving Hillsborough empty handed as Wednesday completed the double over Newcastle.

Defeat cost The Magpies top spot for the first time since February although the failure of Huddersfield and Reading to capitalise on this slip up meant that there was still a 10 point gap to the Play-off places and with one game fewer to go in fact United's hand had strengthened in terms of automatic promotion.

Sheffield Wednesday are a sleeping giant and well supported so the gate of under 30,000 was a surprise for such a big game. Pricey admission was the reason with away fans charged £42 for a game outside the top tier.

Paying supporters got a lot of commitment but not much top quality for their money and had to wait almost an hour for a goal although there was almost an early one when Karl Darlow's crossbar was shaken in the second minute by Gary Hooper's volley. When a goal did come it went to the home side from a set-piece. Defender Tom Lees got on the end of a Ross Wallace free kick to score with a header from 10 yards out. Within 10 minutes United fell further behind, this time to another header, Steven Fletcher arrowing one beyond the despairing Darlow from Daniel Pudil's cross.

While Christian Atsu was quickly brought on to replace Mo Diame, 10 minutes elapsed after the second goal before Benitez decided to roll the dice and introduce Mitrovic for his first action in seven games. The Serb only had 12 minutes to make an impact but provided his admirers with some ammunition by claiming an assist for Jonjo Shelvey's late consolation when Keiren Westwood couldn't hold Mitro's shot, leaving Shelvey to sweep home the rebound.

Shelvey had earlier audaciously gone close with a shot from inside his own half having seen the 'keeper off his line, maybe even thinking of going for an early cuppa as it was so close to half time! Had that gone in it would have been a contender for goal of the season but it was a rare moment of inspiration at a time when the side were more workmanlike than wonderful.

Not for the first time Rafa was concerned about game management, noting, "We didn't manage the situation the way we have to...We were playing with our hearts not our brains."

Hearts did matter though as with the anniversary of the Hillsborough disaster approaching both Newcastle United and former Liverpool boss Benitez leaving wreaths in honour of the 96 who so tragically lost their lives at this stadium.

UNITED: Darlow, Anita, Lascelles, Mbemba, Dummett, Ritchie (Mitrovic 78), Shelvey, Diame (Atsu 72), Gouffran, Perez, Gayle (Murphy 29).

Unused: Elliott, Gamez, Haidara, Ameobi.

Att: 28,883

Referee: Stuart Attwell

Post-match league position: 2nd

NEWCASTLE UNITED 1 LEEDS UNITED 1

St. James'

Good Friday 14th April

SCORERS:

Lascelles	**67**	**1-0**
Wood	90+5	1-1

Newcastle returned to form and did everything but win this game even though they deservedly led four minutes into added time. Leeds were battered as Newcastle mustered 22 shots and 19 corners to Leeds' four and none. "I am pleased with the performance of the team, the commitment, the passion, the effort, but I am disappointed because we make a mistake at the end" said Rafa afterwards.

The visiting Play-off hopefuls did go close early on, Alfonso Pedraza hitting the bar from the edge of the box but after that ninth minute scare it was all Newcastle as the Friday night Sky viewers saw United's determination to move a step closer to finishing the job.

Eventually the break-through arrived mid-way through the second half, skipper Jamaal Lascelles' seeing his effort just go over the line after the recalled Aleksandar Mitrovic had a hand in the goal by heading Yoan Gouffran's cross into the danger area.

Leeds were pinned back throughout, Shelvey and Ritchie constantly putting their rear-guard under pressure while Gouffran hit the post as well as having a hand in the goal.

Newcastle had produced far inferior displays to this and won but had victory snatched away here in the fifth minute of added time to highlight that especially in the closing stages of a season it is points that matter not performances. Suddenly those dour games against Burton and Wigan looked all the more pleasing.

Right at the death ex-Oxford winger Kemar Roofe delivered a cross from which the Championship's top scorer Chris Wood snatched his 25th goal of the season. The New Zealand international had been starved of service but took his chance when it came to take Leeds into fourth place but allow Brighton to suddenly open up a four-point gap on Newcastle with four games to go.

UNITED: Darlow, Anita, Lascelles, Mbemba, Dummett, Ritchie (Yedlin 84), Shelvey, Hayden (Colback 79), Gouffran, Perez (Diame 90), Mitrovic.

Unused: Elliott, Hanley, Atsu, Murphy

Attendance: 52,301

Referee: Chris Kavanagh

Post-match league position: 2nd

RUN IN RECKONING

Leeds' late, late leveller looked to have been the deciding factor in the race for the title. Barring disaster both Newcastle and Brighton realised that the pair of them were going up but the battle to get their hands on the championship trophy had seen a tight contest. Suddenly though a four-point gap had opened up with only four games to go. Chris Hughton's Seagulls were clearly in pole position to take the title to the south coast.

Huddersfield's win over Preston had seen them narrow the gap to Newcastle potentially to five points if they won their game in hand. Given The Magpies goal difference of +39 to Huddersfield's +5 though Newcastle knew two more wins from their last four games would seal promotion. It was a case of holding their nerve and having the determination to try and still overtake the leaders.

Brighton still had to entertain lowly Wigan Athletic and Bristol City as well as travelling to the teams who had come down with Newcastle a year earlier: Norwich City and Aston Villa on the final day.

The Magpies meanwhile faced long trips to Ipswich Town and Cardiff City and had Preston North End and Barnsley to welcome to St. James' – The Tykes being the final day opposition.

Huddersfield had trips to Derby, Wolves and desperate Birmingham to negotiate and tricky Fulham at home with Cardiff at the John Smith's Stadium on the final day. Prior to their victory over Preston, Huddersfield had lost five of the previous eight games. The Terriers didn't appear to have the bite to close the gap on Newcastle but they couldn't be discounted – just as Leeds couldn't be in the fifth minute of injury time.

IPSWICH TOWN 3   NEWCASTLE UNITED 1

Portman Road

Easter Monday 17th April

SCORERS:

Sears	41	0-1
Murphy	**62**	**1-1**
McGoldrick	69	1-2
Huws	90+3	1-3

It was a good job so much good work had gone in earlier in the season as Newcastle stuttered towards the finishing line. If a 46 game promotion campaign was a marathon not a sprint, United were breathing heavily and requiring refreshment for the last few yards. Maybe if Benitez had been backed in January when he wanted Andros Townsend an added outlet might have helped at this stage – as well as already preparing for the step up in class.

Defeat at Ipswich meant eight points had been dropped out of the last nine. The Seagulls were disappearing over the horizon – having mathematically guaranteed promotion and now being seven points clear of United with just nine to play for, with Newcastle's long superior goal difference now wiped out.

A draw for Huddersfield narrowed the gap but not by much and in fact Reading were now in third place. They were the only two sides who could mathematically catch Newcastle and it still looked unlikely – but were United to take just one point from the next three games as they had from the last three they could conceivably be in trouble. It was worrying and more than a blip, the only wins in the last eight games had been narrow home victories against struggling sides but now it was Newcastle who were struggling and for the first time in a year more than two goals were conceded in the league away from home. In a campaign where the away form had been terrific this was also the first time consecutive away trips had seen the Toon Army return empty handed.

Right from the start of the season Newcastle had had few bad habits. One of them was leaking goals just before the break and they did so again here with Freddie Sears under a minute after Matt Ritchie had gone close at the other end with a spectacular diving header.

Benitez had banked on Daryl Murphy marking his return to Portman Road and the striker who had been the top scorer in the Championship with Ipswich two seasons earlier didn't disappoint. The 34 year old Irish international gave United parity just past the hour but before United could benefit from that goal and get on top, Sears tore into them again. This time he was the provider, creating an opportunity for David

McGoldrick to restore the Suffolk side's lead. Goalkeeper Karl Darlow evidently didn't take to the East Anglian air. At Norwich two months earlier his attempted clearance gave away a goal scored by Cameron Jerome and here another poor kick resulted in United falling behind again.

Although Mick McCarthy blustered, "It was our best performance of the season" Ipswich weren't fantastic although they hadn't needed to be to defeat a hesitant and seemingly nervous Newcastle.

An injury time goal had proved costly against Leeds and another was conceded here at Ipswich but by then United were taking chances by pushing forward for an equaliser leaving former Manchester City youngster Emyr Huws to put a gloss on the score-line from the home point of view.

On a day dedicated as 'Sir Bobby Robson Day' by Ipswich, no doubt Sir Bobby would have been saddened by how far two of the teams he loved had fallen and he wouldn't have been alone as Benitez admitted, "I am concerned about the change in my team's performance from Leeds on Friday to the performance today. We all know we have to win our games and now we have to change and improve."

UNITED: Darlow, Yedlin (Gamez 78), Lascelles, Hanley, Dummett, Atsu, Shelvey, Hayden (Gouffran 61), Ritchie (Mitrovic 82), Diame, Murphy.

Unused: Elliott, Mbemba, Colback, Perez.

Att: 25,684

Referee: Tim Robinson

Post-match league position: 2nd

NEWCASTLE UNITED 4 PRESTON NORTH END 1

St. James'

Monday 24th April

SCORERS:

Perez	7	**1-0**
Hugill	14	1-1
Atsu	45	**2-1**
Ritchie	65p	**3-1**
Perez	67	**4-1**

Worried comments coming back from Ipswich had developed into feverish bar-room chat, panic calls to phone–ins and social media meltdown for some as the prospect of United blowing it was raised as a possibility. Nerves were frayed as Newcastle had been the best side in the league for most of the year with only Brighton laying alternative claim for that title.

The two-horse race to see who would get their hands on the championship trophy had been an interesting side-show but with the front two having been the top two for six months it had seemed almost settled that the pair would go up together, like the Brownlee brothers crossing the line together with it not mattering massively which one of them broke the tape first, as long as the Promised Land was reached.

Since the trip to Portman Road the Promised Land looked like it might have been down a turn-off Newcastle had missed. They might need to turn around and have another go at finding it before the chasing pack caught up and beat them to it.

Newcastle's next and penultimate home game was on a Monday night by which time Brighton could have sewn up the title by winning their Friday night fixture. More worryingly Huddersfield might have tightened Tyneside nerves a bit more should they win their own weekend fixture.

However by the time referee Andy Madley blew the first whistle for The Magpies' next game the fat lady could be heard starting to sing. What a weekend it had been and Newcastle hadn't even kicked off.

Firstly Brighton goalkeeper David Stockdale had done his bit by scoring not one but two own goals as his side lost 2-0 at Norwich on the Friday night. The former Darlington goalie failed to get his hat-trick but freakishly twice saw efforts from Alex Pritchard come back off the frame of the goal and rebound in off him. Even better news came on the Saturday afternoon as Huddersfield were given a taste of the medicine Newcastle had been force fed the previous month. Steaming into the Play-offs Fulham travelled to Huddersfield and handed out a 4-1 hammering that effectively ended any hopes the Yorkshire club had of going up automatically. This propped the door to the Premier League wide open for Newcastle.

United needed just three points and had three games to get them. They hadn't been in good form but after the opening two defeats, had fans been offered the scenario that now faced the team it would have been grabbed. Now the question was could the team grab the win they needed?

Opponents Preston were slap bang in the middle of the table with nothing to play for and of course had already been to St. James' in the League Cup and smashed for six. True their league line-up had put up more of a fight on their own patch but clearly North End were brittle and offered Rafa's revivalists a glorious opportunity to finish the job. Even the referee was the same as for the League Cup visit of Preston and although he reportedly is a Huddersfield supporter he reduced Preston to ten men as he had on their cup visit.

If Newcastle displayed some of their bad habits at Ipswich they were on their best behaviour here. Amongst their good habits had been scoring early goals and this was as good as time as any to get one, just to soothe any jangling nerves that the team might freeze on the big occasion, Perez providing the finishing touch when Preston prevaricated over clearing a seventh minute corner.

Unfortunately as so often happened during the course of the season an early tonic wasn't capitalised on and the visitors equalised just seven minutes later thanks to one time Gateshead man Jordan Hugill who traded passes with Tom Barkhuizen before beating Rob Elliott from 10 yards.

Elliott's inclusion was a typically big call by Rafa the Gaffer. The Republic of Ireland international keeper hadn't played since being injured on international duty over a year earlier but Benitez believed in him enough to ask him to make his come-back in such an important game. Because they had been the better side much more often than not Newcastle's deficiencies in the goalkeeping department had been disguised. Matz Sels had started the season as first choice and while Benitez had persisted with him as he tried to adapt to the English game having arrived from AA Gent in Belgium, it was patently obvious that neither the defence or the crowd had confidence in him. Sels never played in the league from September and not at all after the cup elimination at Oxford. For the bulk of the season Karl Darlow had been the trusted custodian and the former Forest man had enjoyed some good games but after one error too many he now found himself benched for the biggest games as Elliott got the nod.

Eager but edgy when it came to re-taking the lead, United had to be patient. Preston were determined to put on a better show than their previous visit but it seemed a case of when, not if, Newcastle would get the goal that would seal promotion. Ironically after conceding so many goals just before hearing Rafa's reflections at the interval United got one of their own.

Isaac Hayden had impressed many throughout the season but the England Under 21 international hadn't managed a full 90 minutes since returning from two months out. With many already heading for the concourse Hayden hit Preston on the break, finding Aleksandar Mitrovic who excellently played in Christian Atsu. The on loan Chelsea man clinically despatched the chance to put Newcastle back in the driving seat and once back in the lead United glided through the gears to the finishing line.

Preston were never really in it after falling behind for a second time and certainly not after going down to 10 men. Hayden looked like getting a goal of his own following a 65th minute corner only for Paul Gallacher to ridiculously handle on the line. The experienced Scotland international must have known that the offence couldn't be missed and he'd be sent off in addition to a penalty award. By the time he'd got into the shower after his red card Preston were 4-1 not 3-1 down as two minutes after Ritchie tucked away the spot kick Perez made it four from another corner as Preston were overwhelmed.

The party got started between the third and fourth goals. Chants of 'We're going up' followed by a repertoire of Rafa chants commenced as the reality of roaring back to the top flight sank in and any lingering nerves floated away over the rooftops.

With quarter of the game still to play there was every possibility that the League Cup score against the same opponents would be at least equalled, but after punishing Preston with 10 goals in two trips to Tyneside United declared and were happy to see the game out safe in the knowledge that promotion was secured. It was the first time since Stan Anderson's side of 1965 that promotion had been clinched in front of a home crowd. Although known as The Spectres back in 1965 rock band Status Quo were already going and it was their 'Rockin' all over the world' that blared out over the stadium loudspeakers as Rafa Benitez came out to salute the crowd. It was a song also heard at Plymouth when under Chris Hughton United clinched the championship and sent Argyle down in 2010.

Relief more than delight was the over-riding emotion for many. Under Rafa Newcastle simply had to get back into the big league at the first opportunity and despite one or two late season hiccups that is what they had succeeded in doing. Now there were two more fixtures to enjoy. The pressure was totally off but there was still something to play for – if they could overtake Brighton the championship trophy would be the cherry on top of what had been a successful season.

UNITED: Elliott, Anita, Lascelles, Clark, Dummett, Ritchie, Hayden, Shelvey, (Colback 76), Atsu (Gouffran 68) Perez (Murphy 83), Mitrovic.

Unused: Darlow, Yedlin, Mbemba, Diame,

Attendance: 50,212

Referee: Andy Madley

Post-match league position: 2nd

CARDIFF CITY 0 NEWCASTLE UNITED 2

Cardiff City Stadium

Friday 28th April

SCORERS:

| Atsu | 55 | 1-0 |
| Hayden | 65 | 2-0 |

Over 4000 travelled to South Wales on a Friday night for a match they could have watched in the pub, when the only thing at stake was keeping Brighton in sight and the historical footnote of a new club record number of away wins if three more points could be garnered. Even victory though would only delay the south coast side the title for under 24 hours provided they won their home game against Bristol City on the Saturday afternoon.

Occupying the thoughts of the Toon Army on the long journey was the question, "Are we really up?" Nothing has ever been simple when it comes to Newcastle United so just a couple of days after the Preston promotion party came news of a Revenue & Customs investigation that affected Newcastle United and West Ham. Details at the time were sketchy and the absence of information fuelled speculation that if found guilty of HMRC offences possibly points could be docked and maybe, just maybe promotion would be snatched away in the corridors of bureaucracy – as had happened to Swindon in 1990 when somehow Sunderland went up instead. Reportedly Newcastle were under investigation regarding a suspected income tax and national insurance fraud with managing director Lee Charnley arrested, although he was quickly released without charge.

At least Newcastle were playing Cardiff City, a team stuck right in the middle of the table with no chance of reaching the play offs or going down so they would be placid opponents… except the Bluebirds these days were managed by Neil Warnock.

The former Hartlepool winger now in his 17th managerial job. Loathe him or loathe him, Warnock is an effective manager. Safe now in mid-table, Cardiff had been one of the bottom when they called for him in October and having won their last three home games Warnock wanted to sign off in front of his own fans with the scalp of Premier bound (hopefully) Newcastle.

Cardiff however never left a meaningful mark on United's goal in which 'keeper Rob Elliott was captaining a side missing several players resting injuries and Matt Ritchie who missed the final two games through suspension.

Although there wasn't a lot of excitement in the game there were two excellent goals. Christian Atsu showed Premier League quality with his 55th minute free kick while 10 minutes later Isaac Hayden scored a cracker from outside the box to ensure a new club record of 14 away wins and a happy journey home as so many had been throughout the season.

For many in the Toon Army though there was the benefit of the fact a Friday night game meant they had the opportunity to explore Cardiff's renowned night-life in celebratory mood.

UNITED: Elliott, Yedlin, Mbemba, Clark, Dummett, Perez (Sterry 90), Hayden, Colback (Shelvey 73), Atsu, Diame, Murphy (Mitrovic 65).

Unused: Darlow, Lazaar, Haidara, Gouffran

Attendance: 23,153

Referee: Graham Scott

Post-match league position: 2nd

NEWCASTLE UNITED 3 BARNSLEY 0

St. James'

Sunday 7th May

SCORERS:

Perez	23	1-0
Mbemba	59	2-0
Gayle	90	3-0

A Sunday lunch-time kick-off brought Barnsley north, hoping not to be shown to be Yorkshire puddings on a day when Newcastle's rise to the top came to a climax. Newcastle needed to better Brighton's result at Aston Villa, but regardless of how Brighton fared this was a day of celebration, one where Newcastle wanted to sign off with a win. If Brighton won too, well promotion was the aim and achieving it would be celebrated. However if Brighton slipped up Newcastle had to be in a position to take advantage so a professional job was required, especially as one particularly significant supporter was attending his first home match of the season – owner Mike Ashley.

Ayoze Perez certainly wanted a winner's medal. He put United ahead half-way through the first half and it was from his shot just before the hour mark that Chancel Mbemba buried a rebound to make it 2-0 against the tiring Tykes. So far so good and with Brighton all square at Steve Bruce's Aston Villa Newcastle were on course to be champions.

In total control of events at St. James', what happened at Villa Park was beyond them so when news filtered through that not only had Glenn Murray put Brighton ahead at Villa with a penalty, but that Villa had also been reduced to ten men it looked as if that was that. United would have to be content with the special trophy now produced by the Football League for runners' up, rather than the magnificent traditional league championship trophy that seemed destined for the south coast.

To be champions Newcastle needed a favour from Brucie's boys and who else should go close but Henri Lansbury. Had he headed home a great chance instead of heading over the bar what an irony that would have been if the man who was Toon Army enemy number one had been the player to allow The Toon to finish on top. Dear old Henri though had already contributed one goal to the United cause and couldn't manage another.

At St. James' Barnsley 'keeper Adam Davies was doing his best to keep the score down, denying Atsu, Haidara and Colback who all looked to get in on the act while he needed his post to thwart Shelvey.

As the final minutes of a league season lasting 4,140 minutes of playing time ticked down Dwight Gayle scored Newcastle's 100th goal of the campaign to wrap up three more points, taking the tally to an excellent 94 – more than two points a game and with it runners' up spot.

Except...coming through from Villa was the news that Jack Grealish had scored a late equaliser against Brighton. Once a Notts County player Grealish was a magpie of sorts and now he was definitely an honorary one. Brighton had blown it, one point from their final three games while Newcastle had bagged nine out of nine had seen Newcastle top the table when it mattered most.

Newcastle United were champions. Their next match would be in the Premier League. Rafa Benitez had stuck with the Toon and taken the Toon Up.

UNITED: Elliott, Yedlin, Hayden (Haidara 13), Mbemba, Dummett, Atsu, Shelvey (Diame 72), Colback, Gouffran, Perez (Gayle 80), Mitrovic.

Unused: Darlow, Anita, Lazaar, Murphy

Attendance: 52,276

Referee: James Linington

Post-match league position: 1st

CHAPTER 12
PROMOTION PARTY

The best parties have a good reason behind them. The reason for this one was so good there were two Tyneside parties after the Preston and Barnsley games, not forgetting the 4,000 strong decampment to Cardiff in between.

The whole point of the season had been to win promotion so the party got started once Preston were packed off to the tune of 4-1. Just 348 days after relegation United were back, mathematically certain of being in the Premier League.

Players win games and there's no doubt that the likes of Ciaran Clark, Dwight Gayle, Andy Ritchie and Jonjo Shelvey to name but four had played massive parts in taking the Toon Up, but head and shoulders above everyone else's contribution was Rafa Benitez.

Rafa had got the best out of everyone all season, both on the pitch and off it as behind the scenes his infectious enthusiasm and attention to detail had inspired and lifted everyone connected to the club. No matter how apparently insignificant a person's role they were aware that the man leading them was someone with a global profile and that he was relying on them to do their bit.

As befits a leader of genuine confidence Rafa did not want to milk the praise for himself but share it for a job well done. "I'm really proud of everyone. I want to congratulate all players, staff and fans" insisted Benitez.

Having won the Champions League with Liverpool and trophies in Spain, Italy and England, Rafa realised how special the Toon Army were, explaining, "The fans have been amazing with me. Their loyalty and everything it means to being a top team like this, with the city behind you. That is why I decided to stay and now I am even happier than before I made that decision."

Having previously twice guided teams to promotion in Spain with Extremadura in 1997-8 and Tenerife in 2000-01, Benitez had seen those teams rise in station for finishing second and third in the Segunda Division. With a minute or so of the season remaining it looked as if promotion as runners' up would be added as a footnote to Rafa's stellar record.

Rivals Brighton had one hand tightly gripping the coveted trophy. They had got themselves into a position where having sealed their own promotion they needed just two points from three games to guarantee the trophy, regardless, of what Newcastle could do. While United kept winning after securing promotion the south coast club faltered. Right at the death Jack Grealish's equaliser against them at Aston Villa meant that for the rest of time the respective club records of Newcastle United and Brighton and Hove Albion would state that it was Newcastle and not Brighton who were the Championship champions for 2017.

Suddenly at St. James' an atmosphere that was one of delight became one of delirium. United had been the best team in the division all season and suddenly they were going to have the trophy to prove it. Brighton had been excellent adversaries but Newcastle had beaten them home and away so there could be no doubt who was the better side.

Behind the scenes, some of those staff Rafa rated so highly suddenly had to quickly unearth and assemble a stage which read Skybet EFL CHAMPIONS 2017, rather than one that they might have expected to have to put together which read 'Promoted 2017'. Newcastle were going up anyway before Grealish's Brighton buster but all of a sudden they were going up as champions.

The previous weekend as the travelling Toon Army partied in the Principality following the Friday night victory at Cardiff, the Championship trophy had been at The Amex Stadium in Brighton, waiting to be presented to The Seagulls had they sewn up the title in front of their own fans instead of slipping up at the hands of Bristol City. The south coast club had given it the works with the Poet in Residence and operatic soprano Donna-Marie Hughes performing 'Abide With Me'.

They should have known better after the infamous 'And Smith must score' moment in the 1983 FA Cup final, a moment that will haunt them forever as Gordon Smith failed to score in the dying seconds of extra time and they were duly beaten 4-0 in the replay against Manchester United a few days later.

Unfortunately for Brighton the lyrics to the cup final hymn 'Abide With Me' include the line, 'Earth's joys grow dim, its glories pass away' and that was certainly the case for them as following Bristol's surprise win the trophy was packed up again and sent to Tyneside.

Some wondered whether on the final day of the season the trophy would be held somewhere half-way between the 205 miles which separate St. James' from Villa Park, ready to head off in the direction of whichever team came out on top. Had that been the case and the driver or pilot of whatever was being used to transport the trophy decided to get a head start and head off to Villa when Brighton seemed destined to be champs, they would have had to make a speedy about-turn when Grealish popped up with his oh so golden goal.

However had Brighton got the result they required the plan was not to present them with it at the home of Villa but at the civic reception they had planned to celebrate their promotion. Had that proved to be the case someone would have had the job of spiriting the championship trophy out of St. James' Park, with probably only a select few people ever knowing the grand old trophy had even been present at St. James'. Thankfully though over 50,000 black and whites were about to see it presented to Newcastle United.

Once the stage building preparations were in place legendary 1969 Fairs Cup winning skipper Bob Moncur, accompanied by representatives from the EFL, carried the trophy onto the pitch before Rafa Benitez became the first man to be awarded his title winning medal.

Subsequently the players were called out by MC Justin Lockwood. Appearing in alphabetical order allowed Rolando Aarons to be first up. The young winger's season had ended horribly with an injury in the EFL Cup game with Cheltenham back in August after a bright start when the then 20 year old appeared to be going to play a regular role as part of Newcastle's squad. Aarons had been one of the scorers in the 5-1 thrashing of Tottenham as Newcastle signalled to the Premier League that their absence would be a short one and now Rolando knew that when he next got into United's league side it would be back in with the big boys.

Aarons' role in the championship triumph had been a small one but 30 players had played their part, big or small. Rafa's rotation had illustrated that the league had been won by the squad not just the regulars. Rob Elliott for instance had played fewer games than Aarons but he'd been ready when called upon, had even captained the side and was part of the success story.

Players such as Daryl Murphy and Grant Hanley had been brought in because of their experience at this level. Between them they had played fewer league games than Vurnon Anita but each could look at their contribution and know they had played their part.

A dozen players had played in 30 or more of the 46 league fixtures with top scorer Dwight Gayle ecstatic over the fact he was about to go home with a Championship medal "It's my favourite season and my favourite end to a season" he enthused. "Winning things is the most important thing and the fact we won the Championship is a great achievement. We're all buzzing about it. It was a fantastic day for us and the fact we managed to do it in the end was a great feeling. It was a big thing for the players, the coaching staff and the fans as well."

Captain Jamaal Lascelles lifted the trophy as the sound of Queen's 'We are the Champions' reverberated around the stadium which was once more a Premier League venue.

As a lap of honour, complete with the players' children and club staff, made its way around the ground the hard work that had been put in since the big kick-off almost exactly nine months ago had provided a re-birth for the club and restored belief amongst its supporters.

It was at this point that the fact that all of the day's championship games had kicked off early suddenly seemed like a good idea. There would be plenty of time to enjoy a few drinks and party the rest of the day and night away. Times like this don't come around on Tyneside nearly often enough and everyone was determined to make the absolute most of it. What was going to be a continuation of the promotion party which had begun at the Preston game was now a championship party and so much the better for that.

As the evening progressed, players and club staff made their way to their promotion party at the Vermont Hotel in the city centre where the champagne corks popped and the panoramic views across the River Tyne had never looked better.

Of the 30 teams to drop out of the top flight in the previous ten seasons only Newcastle themselves, WBA, Birmingham City and Burnley had succeeded in winning instant automatic promotion, although four others had returned instantly via the Play-offs. On the other hand, 11 had failed to even finish in the top 10 in their first year after the drop, with Wolves following up propping up the Premier League in 2011-12 by being relegated again in 2012-13.

Newcastle though had bucked the trend as they had in 2009-10 under Chris Hughton who having seen his old club pip his new one to the title showed his undoubted class by saying, "I'd like to congratulate Newcastle on a wonderful season. They've just beaten us to it. I think the two best teams this season are the two who have gone up automatically."

While Hughton's Albion intended to parade the Championship trophy around Brighton having never won such a high division before, Newcastle never had any intention of taking the trophy on a bus tour of Tyneside. Politely turning down the City Council's offer of a parade former Champions League winner Benitez had remarked, "You have to celebrate but maybe you don't need to do a parade in the city. You can celebrate though and then look to the future."

Maybe the time to find an open topped bus for Newcastle will be when they have won a more major trophy under Rafa. Should the Toon ever do that they will be hard pressed to come up with a finale more amazing than when the winning goal was scored in the dying seconds 200 miles away.

Chapter 13

PLAYER OF THE YEAR

CIARAN CLARK

Goal-scorers rightly grab the glory and hog the headlines. Eye-catching creative midfielders can have people waxing lyrical over their vision and range of passing, and sometimes goalkeepers can be the hero on days where they are required to produce acrobatic displays to the delight of the photographers.

When it comes to choosing a player of the season though, an assessment of the value of an individual to the team over the sustained period of an entire campaign is needed. While from the outside looking in the goals of Dwight Gayle, the verve of Matt Ritchie or the panache of Jonjo Shelvey might at first glance be the key ingredient in the success of Benitez's champions, it was centre back Ciaran Clark who emerged as the most important member of the side.

Gayle's goal tally would undoubtedly have been even more impressive had injuries not disrupted his season after the former Palace man had reached 20 by January but without him United still did well enough up front to register a century of goals in the season. Similarly, Shelvey and Ritchie were brilliant in tandem but if one of them was missing the side could still look to the other when in need of a creative spark.

In Clark's case though his absence was more telling. While Newcastle looked well stocked for central defenders when Ciaran was signed at the start of the season, it soon became apparent that as a pivot he was the man a top team missed most of all if he was absent. As at Manchester City where a five-star cast of forwards could cope with ease if one of them was missing, but the loss of Vincent Kompany could be costly, Newcastle seemed to be a little less United without their best defender.

Facts backed this opinion. Newcastle lost as many times in the dozen games Clark missed than in the 34 he played.

WITH CLARK:	P	W	D	L
	34	24	5	5

WITHOUT CLARK	P	W	D	L
	12	5	2	5

While some other central defenders knew what was in store for them in the championship, all of Clark's experience going into the season was in the Premier League. The more robust, relentlessly physical aspects of the EFL proved to be no problem for him as he adapted so well that he relished the battles that came his way. Time after time he stood head and shoulders above those around him through his commanding presence, composure and above all the pace that he brought to what could at other times be a sluggish central defence, as illustrated in the defeat at Ipswich for instance. A good talker and organiser, Clark's inclusion always made the defence look more together as a unit as he coaxed them through each match. With what he's learning from Benitez there's a future manager in Clark.

Signed on the same day as Mo Diame, Clark arrived once pre-season preparations had been completed with Rafa describing Ciaran as, "A very versatile player" adding, "As a left-footed centre back he can also play left back and as a defensive midfielder." Given time to get to know the squad Clark came into the side for the third game of the season and helped to make an immediate difference as the first points of the season were acquired, after two defeats reminded everyone that promotion wasn't going to be handed to Newcastle on a plate.

Clark's eve of season departure from Aston Villa annoyed Villa boss Roberto Di Matteo who raged at the release clauses in his squad's contracts after also losing Senegal international midfielder Idrissa Gana Gueye to Everton. "Fundamentally there shouldn't be a buy-out clause. If you have to give it then you certainly shouldn't do it for this amount of transfer fee" argued the Italian, who had seen Newcastle secure Clark for what he viewed as a bargain £5m when the player was reportedly just one year into a five year deal he had with the midlands outfit.

The fee indeed did prove to be a bargain for a player who having apparently been hit with a 50% wage reduction following Villa's relegation was prepared to look for a new challenge, away from the club he had grown up with since first becoming attached to them when just 11 years old.

Having just returned from playing at Euro 16 with the Republic of Ireland, Clark accepted the chance to move to Newcastle having helped Villa to what proved to be a costly goalless draw for The Toon at Villa Park. That match proved to be his final competitive appearance for his boyhood club.

Although he had represented the Republic of Ireland at the Euro's, Harrow born Clark had previously played for England at four different age groups, winning the final two of his 19 England junior caps at Under 20 level before deciding to represent the country of his parents' birth. To the immense pride of his family, most of whom live in Leitrim, Clark was first named in an Ireland squad in November 2010, Ciaran made his senior bow for the Republic the following February. Capped 19 times while with Villa, Clark won five more caps during his first season with Newcastle. The first of these came in a friendly against Oman less than a month after joining the club, quickly followed by a World Cup draw in Serbia. That match in Belgrade saw him come up against new club mate Aleksandar Mitrovic while another new club mate, Daryl Murphy got a late equaliser for the Irish with his first international goal.

Now a Premier League player again, Clark is a key player for his country as well as his club although the knee injury which ruled him out of the final game of the season against Barnsley also forced him to miss the Republic's summer friendlies with Mexico and Uruguay along with their important World Cup qualifier against Austria.

By his own admission Clark is a better defender now than the one who went down with Aston Villa. At the age of 27 he is coming into what should be the peak years for a centre-back and acknowledges the role Rafa has played in improving him as a footballer. "It has been a total change for me, Rafa Benitez is a real man-manager and he wants you to get involved and learn" explained the man who was given his league debut in 2009 by his current international boss Martin O'Neill. Subsequently at Villa Clark played under: Gerard Houllier, Alex McLeish, Paul Lambert, Tim Sherwood, Remi Garde, Eric Black and in friendlies at least, Roberto Di Matteo.

Benefiting from Benitez's tuition, Clark continued, "He wants to teach you and improve you as a player – if he does that then it improves the team. He works hard on defensive shape and positional stuff, it's something I have probably not had as a player in my career. I feel like I am learning so much and hopefully I can keep doing it, I feel like I have learned more about the game."

Like any good player of course Clark keeps learning. First involved in the Premier League when debuting a month before his 20th birthday in 2009 when helping Villa to a clean sheet in beating Fulham, he was well enough thought of to be handed a contract extension shortly afterwards, but wouldn't play again for a year. Again he helped achieve a clean sheet in a home win before making his away debut a week later – at St. James'.

Clark quickly found out what St. James' could be like as he was on the wrong end of a 6-0 hammering, Andy Carroll grabbing a hat-trick. Quite possibly the impression left on the youngster that day might have made the later prospect on being on the right side of The Toon Army when the place was bouncing, an appealing one. What doesn't kill you makes you stronger though and Clark went on to really establish himself at Villa for whom he played regularly and chipped in with four goals, including a brace against Arsenal.

Defenders who can contribute with the occasional goal are a bonus to any team and in winning the Player of the Year award in the promotion season Clark contributed three goals. Making hay while the sun shone Ciaran joined in with the free for all in the 6-0 at QPR and also notched against Brentford and Bristol City at St. James'. The Tyneside citadel had witnessed his first goal there back in September 2012 in a 1-1 draw for Villa, while later that season Clark got his first senior international goal, a winner against Poland in Dublin.

As the Premier League beckons there is no doubt that Rafa Benitez will overhaul his Championship winning squad. Just as he re-shaped the side which went down into one equipped to go up, the Gaffer will look to assemble a squad ready for the challenges ahead. Such is the nature of professional football that not everyone who took the Toon up will be able to continue on the next part of the journey but there can be little doubt that in Player of the Year Ciaran Clark United Benitez has a bedrock of the defence he can count on.

PFA CHAMPIONSHIP TEAM OF THE SEASON

Sponsored by Panini

While those who watched Newcastle every week chose Ciaran Clark as their Player of the Year, it was three other United players who made it into the PFA Championship Team of the season.

Clark's centre-back partner Jamaal Lascelles earned selection, as did midfield maestro Jonjo Shelvey and goal machine Dwight Gayle. Partnering Lascelles in the XI ahead of Clark was Brighton's impressive Lewis Dunk while in addition to the raised eyebrows concerning Clark's omission there was added amazement at the absence of Matt Ritchie.

Indeed the champions had one player fewer chosen than runners' up Brighton, with two Fulham players selected along with one each from Huddersfield and Leeds.

DAVID STOCKDALE (Brighton & Hove Albion)

Outstanding goalkeeper who missed only one game but bizarrely scored two own goals in The Seagulls third last game at Norwich, which opened the door to Newcastle overtaking Brighton in the title chase.

BRUNO (Brighton & Hove Albion)

Like Rafa Benitez, Brighton right back Bruno Saltor Grau had previously been with Valencia who he left to join Brighton in 2012. A measure of his consistency is this was the Spaniard's second successive season in the PFA Team of the Year.

LEWIS DUNK (Brighton & Hove Albion)

Brighton born central defender who missed just three games, scoring in wins over Fulham and Norwich.

JAMAAL LASCELLES (Newcastle United)

A player who blossomed under Benitez, showing the character to know when to stand up and be counted. Captained United to the title.

RYAN SESSEGNON (Fulham)

Still 16 at the end of the season, Sessegnon had a sensational season, not least when scoring twice and winning a penalty when Fulham won at St. James'. The first person born this century to score in the league, this young English player may well follow Newcastle into the Premier League regardless of his club losing in the Play-offs.

TOM CAIRNEY (Fulham)

With 13 goals and 11 assists from midfield, 26 year old former Blackburn Player of the Year Tom Cairney became a hot property and one reportedly interesting Newcastle, against whom the Scotland international scored with a 25 yarder at St. James'.

ANTHONY KNOCKAERT (Brighton & Hove Albion)

The EFL Championship Player of the Year was one who got away from Rafa who identified the France Under 21 international winger as a potentially key player and tried to sign him at the start of the season. Rafa was right in his assessment as the former Leicester man scored 15 times in an outstanding season.

AARON MOOY (Huddersfield Town)

Sydney born Aussie Aaron spent the season on loan to Huddersfield from Manchester City and scored against Newcastle at the John Smith's Stadium. Like Cairney, midfielder Mooy is another member of the PFA team of the season reportedly interested in the player for whom Manchester City are reported to have turned down an £8.8m bid for from a Championship club in January.

JONJO SHELVEY (Newcastle United)

Ever since becoming Charlton's youngest ever player under two months after his 16th birthday, Shelvey has been a player teams revolve around. Good enough to be capped by England and be signed by Liverpool. With all the talent in the world, now at the age of 25 Jonjo has the ability to star for Newcastle in the top flight.

DWIGHT GAYLE (Newcastle United)

23 goals in an injury hit season was a fabulous reward for the pace-man whose goals per minutes played record was the best in the division. Shortlisted for the Championship Player of the year award Gayle twice went home with the match ball after hat tricks against Norwich and Birmingham.

CHRIS WOOD (Leeds United)

New Zealand international centre forward whose 27 goals made him the Championship's top scorer. One of three players listed for the Championship Player of the Year award, his equaliser five minutes into added time at St. James' in April threatened to cost Newcastle the title.

CHAPTER 14
TOP 10 MOMENTS

In a season to remember there were many fantastic moments. Following a season of lows 2016-17 was a year of one high after another. How does your top 10 compare with Toon Up's Top 10?

1) RAFA STAYING FOR 2016-17

Everyone likes to be loved. No matter how much money you have in the bank, how big your house is or how flash your car. Liverpool lads The Beatles once told the world 'Money Can't Buy Me Love' and sure enough it was love not lolly that convinced Benitez to stay with the Toon, even though it meant one of the continent's top bosses plying his trade in the second tier.

"The love I could feel from the fans was a big influence in my decision" said the man who had started the season as manager of Real Madrid and was now committing himself to a season facing Barnsley rather than Barcelona. The visit of Barnsley wouldn't turn out too badly though!

Stop for a moment and consider what might have happened had Rafa not felt the love? Who might have taken over? Would they have brought United straight back up? If they had would they have the pulling power of Benitez now a team for the top-flight is required? Make no mistake about it, the most magical moment of the season came before a ball was kicked. Everything else flowed from Rafa staying as the Gaffer.

2) RAFA STAYING FOR 2017-18

Excitement at Newcastle going up was tempered by the worry that they would return without Rafa. In recent seasons United's top flight campaigns had been lukewarm at best. No-one wants a club of Newcastle's size to be also rans, and while no one expects or demands an immediate return to the Keegan quality years there is the hope and belief that with Benitez as boss Newcastle United won't be joining the big boys just to make up the numbers. News that Rafa was to continue was without doubt the best signing the Toon could make regardless of whoever Benitez brings in for the battles ahead.

3) NEWCASTLE UNITED 4 PRESTON NORTH END 1

Just beat a team you've already beaten 6-0 at home and you're up. Simple. It was simple for Brighton to get two points from their last three games to win the league too but they didn't. Nothing is simple in football but you'll know that if you've been following the Toon for long enough.

It looked simple enough when Perez put The lads one up in seven minutes... but seven minutes later Preston were level again to set the nerves jangling. Thankfully Atsu restored the lead just before the half-time assessments but the game could easily still turn.

Almost 20 minutes of the second half had gone with the game still having just one goal in it when Preston's Paul Gallagher took the heat off with the most productive of handballs. Sent off for conceding a penalty converted by Ritchie left Toon 3-1 up against 10 men and Perez chested the ball home to make victory certain a couple of minutes later everyone could stick their chest out that bit further in pride at being back in the Premier League.

4) NEWCASTLE UNITED 4 NORWICH CITY 3

On a Wednesday night with a quarter to eight kick off it was understandable for a few people to drift away with the game deep into injury time. Pace-setters Norwich had taken a 3-1 lead and while that two goal cushion had been halved within a couple of minutes the visitors had just about seen the game out and were about to wrap up the three points and take them back to East Anglia. Over 20 minutes had passed since Dwight Gayle had reduced the deficit to 2-3 and the game seemed to be just about up, in more ways than one.

Suddenly Yoan Gouffran's slightly deflected header nestled in the back of The Canaries net and the points had been shared at the death.

A draw hadn't been wanted at the start of the match but it was more than welcome now. It meant a point added to the total and importantly two taken away from promotion rivals.

What happened next was a forerunner to the bedlam that broke out when Jack Grealish scored for Villa against Brighton on the final day, handing Toon the title. In the circumstances everyone was pleased to have drawn level at the last with Norwich, just as they were pleased with the score-line against Barnsley on the final day, but when somehow Dwight Gayle got the latest of late winners a minute after the equaliser it not only completed his hat-trick but became one of the most dramatic moments of elation the old stadium has witnessed in this or any other season. These are the moments grandchildren not yet born will be told about.

5) JACK GREALISH SCORES FOR ASTON VILLA AGAINST BRIGHTON

Jack Grealish spent the first hour of this game sitting on the bench, little thinking he was about to cause one of the greatest moments of the season 200 miles north. The 21 year old's Great Great grandfather Billy Garraty played against Newcastle in the 1905 FA Cup final helping Villa to win 2-0. Now over a century later Grealish said sorry with his invaluable equaliser.

Holding out against 10 man Villa – who had seen Ciaran Clark's former central defensive partner Nathan Baker sent off – Brighton were a minute away from taking the title when Grealish popped up to score from just inside the box. The hearts and bank balances of the dodgy entrepreneurs outside Villa Park about to sell Brighton Champions 2017 scarves sunk as waves of elation arrived at St. James' where the real champions were playing. Never had a Jack in the box been so welcome.

Grealish was more than welcome when as an old team mate of Ciaran Clark's he was seen soon afterwards on a night out with Dwight Gayle, DeAndre Yedlin, Jamaal Lascelles, Rob Elliott, Grant Hanley and Rolando Aarons all of whom owed him a drink or two!

Toon fan Daniel Wright-Miller had promised to have a tattoo of Grealish on his shin is Grealish scored a winner against Brighton and Newcastle won the league so there's one fan who will always have a special reminder of the day Jack Grealish scored for Newcastle… sort of.

6) BRIGHTON AND HOVE ALBION 1 NEWCASTLE UNITED 2

Newcastle had beaten Brighton in August. Back then it seemed likely that The Seagulls would be big rivals, but there's a long way from August to February, so when Newcastle made the long trek to The Amex Stadium on the last day of that month the match had the look of a showdown about it. The clubs had traded top-spot for months and facing the eventual runners' up away from home was the toughest assignment on the season's fixture list.

That task became even tougher when Albion took an early lead and as the game wore on, an equaliser and a point would have been a cause for delight. Having forced that longed for leveller with under 10 minutes to go it looked like a cracking result but then when Perez popped up with an 89th minute winner it was bedlam in Brighton as suddenly in the space of a few minutes Newcastle had overturned the result in what was effectively a six-pointer.

7) QUEENS PARK RANGERS 0 NEWCASTLE UNITED 6

This was a statement result – a signal to the rest of the Championship that while Newcastle had made an 'iffy' start but had looked to be recovering with four wins on the bounce, this showed they were in full stride now. A 6-0 away win, to a half-way decent side who had spent fortunes in recent seasons, sent shockwaves around the league. Clubs who feared Newcastle were nailed on for one of the two automatic promotion places would take one look at that score-line and think the rest of the table were playing for one place or a Play-off slot from now on.

As it happened Brighton largely kept pace with the two front-runners putting daylight between them and the chasing pack and while there would be the occasional little blip to a large extent United didn't look back after the QPR result. It was the fifth win in a row but the one that said to every other team, watch out because we can destroy you.

8) HUDDERSFIELD 1 NEWCASTLE UNITED 3

Following on from the superb win at Brighton four days earlier, in some respects this match was even more important that what effectively proved to be the title decider with The Seagulls. Huddersfield were the side most likely to threaten the automatic places. If they could win this game they would be only five points behind United with a game in hand. Too close for comfort. If Newcastle could hold them at arm's length with a point apiece then even if The Terriers won their game in hand there would still be an eight point gap and with United having a vastly superior goal difference that would necessitate three defeats in a row with Huddersfield winning three in succession just to draw level.

There was a pre-match boost as before the late kick off for live TV came the news that Brighton had failed to bounce back from the deflation of late defeat by the Toon and had dismally lost 3-0 at Nottingham Forest. Even a draw for Newcastle would therefore extend the lead over the south coast club but Brighton's result was a filip for Huddersfield too. They went into the game knowing victory would give them the chance of pulling up to within three points of the second automatic promotion place and still with that game in hand.

It was absolutely all to play for as the match kicked off at the John Smith's Stadium where Newcastle quickly established control with an early goal and another before half time. Huddersfield though pulled a goal back with 18 minutes to play giving the record home league crowd reason to rouse themselves for a grandstand finish. For a time it was incredibly tense but with the game in injury time substitute Dwight Gayle – helped by some comical goalkeeping – scored to make it 3-1. Wrapping up a fantastic week the moment Gayle's goal it the net provided a huge release of relief.

Surely it was all over now. Surely the fat lady was dusting off her microphone. Suddenly Newcastle had opened up an 11 point gap to third place with just 10 matches to play.

9) NEWCASTLE UNITED 2 BRIGHTON AND HOVE ALBION 0

Pre-season confidence had taken a bit of a hit after the false start had given the rest of the league a head start on United. Surprise package Huddersfield had set the pace and already had a points total in double figures after four games, while Brighton had already seamlessly slipped into the other automatic promotion position. Having only missed out on an automatic promotion spot in the previous season on a marginal goal difference it was obvious that Chris Hughton's team would be serious contenders this time round.

Having started with those defeats against Fulham and Huddersfield, wins had been registered against Reading and Bristol City so the visit of Brighton was to be the Litmus test as to how ready United were to surge up the table. Two set pieces and a handy red card to the red shirted visitors later and suddenly Newcastle were not only in the Play-off places for the first time but they were above Brighton and just two points off the automatic places. As Jonjo Shelvey's first goal for the club hit the back of the net to open up a two goal lead against opponents already reduced to 10 men, belief re-ignited in the black and white army with chants of 'We're gonna win the league' belted out before the bars were hit on what was going to be a good night with many more to follow.

10) LEEDS UNITED 0 NEWCASTLE UNITED 2

It's always nice to beat Leeds, regardless of the circumstances and this was the first visit to Elland Road since 2003-04. Leeds have fallen a long way since the days when they were a power in the land but under former Swansea boss Garry Monk they were building a bit of momentum and the home fans in a packed stadium fancied their chances of preventing United from chalking up a club record equalling ninth win in a row.

They didn't.

Newcastle haven't lost at Leeds this century and had no intention of doing so here as a comprehensively professional performance provided a comfortable win that featured goals from the sublime to the cor blimey. One time England 'keeper Rob Green has fallen as far as Leeds and his laughable butterfingers at dropping a ball at Gayle's feet was a gift it would have been rude not to accept. Gayle's second though was a wonderful team goal that amply illustrated to Leeds' biggest gate of the season why Newcastle would go up as champions while they wouldn't even reach the Play-offs.

CHAPTER 15
TOP 10 GOALS

With 100 goals scored there was a treasury of goal-den moments to pick from during 2016-17. How many of Toon-up's favourites would make your top 10? Goals here are chosen on the basis of how good they were not how important they were.

1) YOAN GOUFFRAN
V WOLVERHAMPTON WANDERERS (H) 2-0

VOLLEY

ASSIST: MATT RITCHIE

In terms of technique this was a goal Bayern Munich would have been thrilled with if it was scored by a combination of Arjen Robben and Robert Lewandowski. In the Robben role Matt Ritchie burst down the right, but got his head up to take a look at the movement racing towards the box as he delivered a right foot cross on the run. Coming in on the far side of the box Yoan Gouffran met the incoming cross full on the volley for a goal that would not have been out of place in a Champions League final. An absolutely brilliant and spectacular goal.

2) DWIGHT GAYLE V NORWICH CITY (H) 4-3

CLINICAL FINISH

ASSIST: JONJO SHELVEY

If this match was great drama, the middle goal of Gayle's hat-trick was the key speech. Jonjo Shelvey made more passes than a night-club Lothario during the season and this was one of the best. Like catching the eye of the stunning blonde on the far side of the dance floor this pass had to score. Dwight Gayle was just the man to make the most of it. Killing the 60 yard ball like a stone he rapidly despatched it for goal that was as inspirational as it was important.

3) DWIGHT GAYLE V BRISTOL CITY (A) 1-0

CONTROL AND FINISH

ASSIST: MO DIAME

Picking up the ball from Chancel Mbemba, Mo Diame carried it across the half-way line before clipping a measured ball into the path of Dwight Gayle. Nipping between two defenders, Gayle glided into position courtesy of a quality first touch and applied the killer second while still on the move. Out of keeping with a turgid game this was a goal of fluid movement.

4) YOAN GOUFFRAN V DERBY COUNTY (A) 2-0

VOLLEY

ASSIST: JONJO SHELVEY

Even professionals are capable of making the kind of goal you can score on the PlayStation look like a deluded attempt at the spectacular on a Sunday morning. This one was no computer generated moment of magic, it was the real thing. Taking a corner from the left hand side Shelvey picked out Gouffran who had found space on the far side of the box. As the ball landed Gouffran pulled the trigger. It was the sort of effort that had it gone wrong the home fans behind the goal would have been ready to guffaw at, but Gouffran's superbly judged shot flew into the corner as The Rams' Johnny Russell on the line was beaten all ends up.

5) DWIGHT GAYLE V BURTON ALBION (A) 2-1

FLICK

ASSIST: MATT RITCHIE

If Bill Shankly was right when he said you needed eight men to carry the piano and three to play it then this goal was an admirable combination of the trio who tinkled the ivories: Shelvey, Ritchie and Gayle. A searching Shelvey ball into the channel was latched onto by Ritchie who sped towards the goal-line before pulling a low ball towards the danger area. Switched on and quicker off the mark than any of the Brewers' defenders, Gayle got a run on them at the near post, deftly delivering the finishing touch with a flick the finest Subbuteo player would be proud of.

6) JONJO SHELVEY V QUEENS PARK RANGERS (A) 6-0

CURLER

ASSIST: AYOZE PEREZ

Jonjo Shelvey gets noticed. Whether it's scoring, delivering inch perfect long passes, hitting the bar from inside his own half or simply making himself the fulcrum of the football his team play, Shelvey never goes back into the dressing room without being a talking point. Even on a night when everyone was on top of their game and the side won 6-0 he had to steal the show. Not only was he the only man to score more than one that night but his second goal, the third of the game, was the pick of the bunch. Coming onto a ball well held up and laid off by Azoze Perez, Shelvey simply took a touch, looked up, picked his spot and curled an effortless shot right into the top corner from outside the box.

7) DARYL MURPHY V ROTHERHAM UNITED (H) 4-0

SWIVEL & SHOT

ASSIST: DEANDRE YEDLIN

Better teams than Rotherham would have struggled to stop this one. Jonjo Shelvey picked out DeAndre Yedlin speeding up the right wing, with the USA international making the most of it by delivering a first time ball into the box. Collecting the cross Daryl Murphy killed it with his first touch by which time he was already swivelling his body so that he could quickly get in a rapid shot which curled into the corner. It was a really slick, well-made and well taken goal.

8) MATT RITCHIE V IPSWICH TOWN (H) 3-0

CURLER

ASSIST: AYOZE PEREZ

Quality goal from a quality player. The former Bournemouth man curled this one in with the outside of his left foot. Winning the ball in the final third Ritchie swapped passes with Perez before putting the gloss on the result with the final goal as he applied his own Matt finish.

9) MATT RITCHIE V BURTON ALBION (H) 1-0

CURLER

ASSIST: JONJO SHELVEY

Not even referee Keith Stroud could find anything wrong with this one. Having earlier bizarrely – and incorrectly – ruled out Ritchie's converted penalty, the ref probably breathed a sigh of relief as Ritchie's decisive goal reduced the repercussions that came the official's way anyway, but would have been much worse if United hadn't won. If promotion – or the title – had been missed by one goal goodness knows what the fall-out would have been?

The goal that did count was worth waiting for though as Ritchie raced towards goal before burying a brilliant right footed curling shot into the top corner.

10) HENRI LANSBURY O.G. V ASTON VILLA (H) 2-0

COMEDY CAPER

ASSIST: TOON ARMY

In a season where everything went right this was in some respects the cherry on the cake. Following his highly controversial display earlier in the season at the City Ground when he was a Nottingham Forest player, the Toon Army were well and truly wound up and ready to give Henri some stick when he duly arrived with Aston Villa following his January transfer move across the midlands. For Lansbury to then suffer the ignominy not just of scoring an own goal but one where he could and should have done much better was to the massive amusement of everyone of a black and white persuasion in the stadium that night. Hard lines Henri !

CHAPTER 16

PREVIOUS PROMOTIONS

2009-10

Slipping out of the Premier League for the first time, it was imperative that Newcastle achieved something they had never done before. That was bounce straight back up at the first attempt – something thankfully they have now done on the last two occasions they have dropped out of the top flight.

Whereas in 2016-17 Chris Hughton was the man managing United's main rivals Brighton, in 2009-10 it was Hughton who was tasked with pulling the club together. He did it magnificently, invariably conducting himself with great dignity, connecting with fans who felt let down and most importantly putting a winning team on the pitch.

A point from eventual runners' up West Brom on the opening day was a decent start. It was brilliantly built on with a run of five successive league wins which took United to the top of the table. After a couple of brief blips which knocked the Magpies off their perch – the second a loss at Scunthorpe – United slipped into overdrive with six successive victories being the beginning of an unbeaten league run stretching over three months.

Defeat at Derby in February was the only loss in the last 33 league games as United totalled a club record 102 points. Promotion became mathematically guaranteed with eight games to spare in a season where no visiting team left St. James' with all three points. With both the best attack and defence in the league, United finished 11 points clear of runners' up West Brom and a massive 23 ahead of third placed Nottingham Forest.

Four players reached double figures in the scoring stakes: Shola Ameobi with 11, Peter Lovenkrands with 16, Kevin Nolan with 18 and Andy Carroll with 19.

1992-93

Kevin Keegan emulated Joe Harvey in managing United to promotion having previously taken them up as captain. In what was the first year of the Premier League Newcastle made sure they joined the party at the first attempt having dropped out of the top flight in 1989.

Special K was leaving nothing to chance as his side stormed to maximum points from the opening 11 games. Having established an impregnable lead United got to the top early and stayed there all season. Even when blips in form arrived such as a run of no wins in six early in the new year, United stayed out in front.

It was a long campaign of over 60 games in total, including half a dozen in the Anglo-Italian Cup which involved trips to Italy in November and December.

David Kelly top scored with 28 goals including a final day hat trick when both he and Andy Cole laid claims to the match ball as Leicester were beaten 7-1, United being 6-0 up at half time.

Like the record purchase of George Lowrie in 1948, the record £1.75m late season buy of Cole was with one eye on the following campaign and the rise in stature. Had Rafa Benitez had the option of bringing in players late in the season with a view to playing in the top flight it would have been fascinating to see who he might have brought in to help finish the job and look to the next stage.

1983-84

With Play-offs yet to be introduced, third place was sufficient to secure promotion under Arthur Cox. Newcastle fully deserved to go up though. They were fully 10 points ahead of fourth placed Manchester City who were beaten 5-0 when they came to Newcastle. The front two of Chelsea and Sheffield Wednesday were well out in front nine points ahead of United. Goal difference gave the London side the trophy but what mattered was that Newcastle returned to the top flight for the first time since 1978.

The story of Newcastle's season centred on captain Kevin Keegan. Teaming up with Peter Beardsley, who had returned from Vancouver Whitecaps, and a young Chris Waddle brought in from the less exotic Tow Law, Newcastle were undoubtedly the most attractive and exciting team around.

The season began well with a 1-0 win at old rivals Leeds where the goal didn't come from one of the star forwards but stalwart John Anderson, a man still enjoying the 2017 promotion as summariser on local radio. Despite that opening day win the season took a little while to get going with Newcastle ninth following a fifth game draw with Grimsby.

The Toon soon climbed the table though, a sequence of six wins taking them to second with the fifth victory of that run being that 5-0 hammering of Manchester City. Significantly on that day all of the goals came from Keegan, Beardsley and Waddle. It was the first time the trio had all scored in the same game, Beardsley getting a hat–trick.

Between them Keegan (28), Beardsley (20) and Waddle (18) score 66 of the 87 goals the side scored that season. Fourth top scorer with seven goals was Terry McDermott who behind the glory of the goal-scorers was so often the man who made the team tick.

1964-65

As in 2017 and 1948 promotion was won at St. James'. Captained by Stan Anderson United won the second division title for the first time. As in 2016-17 the runners' up (Northampton Town) were pipped by a point but there was a gap of seven points between United and third placed Bolton.

A settled side saw six players play at least 40 of the 44 games played, with goalkeeper Gordon Marshall, young defender Frank Clark and 'They Shall Not Pass' defender John McGrath all ever presents.

Flanked by wing halves Anderson and the talented Jim Iley, McGrath was part of a half-back line that the side revolved around.

As in 2016-17 six goals were scored in an away win, this time at Swindon.

Goals flowed at St. James' too where on the third occasion five goals were hit at home, eventual runners' up Northampton were leathered 5-0 as United went to the top of the table for the first time shortly before Christmas.

Once having risen to the top of the tree, Newcastle stayed there, promotion being sealed on Good Friday when just under 60,000 saw Willie Penman and Iley get the goals against Bolton who would finish third and in years to come be managed by skipper Anderson.

Proudly managing the United team was Joe Harvey, the captain of the club's last promotion winners and a man whose finest moment as manager was still to come.

1947-48

Relegated in 1934 when they finished just behind Birmingham, Newcastle went up just behind the same club in the second league season after World War two. Appropriately captain Joe Harvey got the first United goal on the day promotion was won.

New manager George Martin did some Rafa style wheeling and dealing, including paying a club record transfer fee of £18,500 to Coventry for George Lowrie in March as Newcastle splashed the cash to try and ensure they went up.

The season started with a bang as Len Shackleton scored twice as Plymouth Argyle were sent on their long journey home after being walloped 6-1. With Jackie Milburn also in the side crowds were well entertained, and the crowds were massive. A record average of over 56,000 was under 10,000 fewer than the gigantic gate that witnessed the promotion winning game at home to Sheffield Wednesday who would eventually finish fourth after fading and failing to win any of their final five games.

1897-98

Newcastle's first promotion saw them finish runners up to Burnley and in the days of two points for a win United were fully six points clear of third placed Manchester City in what was a season of just 30 fixtures.

That gap was not enough to simply see Newcastle go up though! Play-off games were introduced in 1986-87 but back in these Victorian times a series of 'Test Matches' determined promotion and relegation. The second division was only six years old and the top two in the Second division played a series of Test Matches against the bottom two in the top flight, who were Blackburn Rovers and Stoke. Those clubs had finished level on points in the top flight – amazingly two of five clubs to end joint bottom on 24 points from 30 games!

United began their Test Matches by beating Stoke 2-1 at St. James' before losing the return match by a single goal. A 4-3 defeat at Blackburn left United in a position where regardless of their final match at home to Blackburn they couldn't succeed if Stoke and Burnley ensured a draw which would guarantee both of them success. Inevitably those clubs played out a goalless draw and although United thrashed Blackburn 4-0 it looked as if it would not be sufficient.

The Test Match system was discredited as a result. Consequently for the following season of 1898-99 the first division was extended from 16 to 18 teams meaning that all four of the clubs who had contested the Test Matches would play in the top flight. At the same time the second division was also extended to 18 teams.

Newcastle had won 21 of their 30 league games, scoring exactly twice the 32 goals they conceded. Finishing just behind United the two Manchester clubs and Arsenal, albeit it was then Woolwich Arsenal and the club that became known as Manchester United were then known as Newton Heath. It was a long time ago! Other sides in the division included Gainsborough Trinity, Burton Swifts, Darwen and Loughborough.

Captained by Jimmy Stott, a tough tackler who tragically died young, Newcastle did not have a manager in those days, the side being selected by a committee of directors.

The season began with four wins Willie Wardrope scoring in all of them and totalling seven goals after those opening matches. Like Stott,

Wardrope was a player who sadly passed away in his thirties. A defeat at eventual champions Burnley brought the run to an end with Burnley later becoming the only visiting side to win at St. James, a place where otherwise United achieved a 100% record.

Leading scorer Jock Peddie bagged 19 goals, a figure that included three hat-tricks. Peddie would score twice when Newcastle won their first match in the top flight but that didn't come until November at the 11th time of asking as United propped up the extended table. Thankfully the team got to grips with the higher level and rose to a final position of 13th.

CHAPTER 17

THE NEXT STEP

No matter how well you do in the Championship, it is always a big step up when you-re-enter the Premier League, even if you have only been missing for a season. One thing that typifies Rafael Benitez is his attention to detail. Clearly a deep thinker on the game, Benitez's understanding of the challenges ahead should leave the Toon Army content that no-one could have a clearer approach.

Just as he loaded up his squad to deal with the demands of a 46 game slog to promotion, Rafa will ready his troops for a challenge that will be less about quantity and more about quality.

It would surprise no-one if during the summer some players who have excelled in lifting Newcastle out of the second tier are jettisoned before the Toon take on the big boys. Just as Kevin Keegan peddled top scorer David Kelly when he had won the Player of the Year award after firing United to promotion in 1992-93, players who have served their purpose are likely to be moved on and sold while their stock is high. There is no room for sentiment in football but players who have worn the jersey with pride will always be assured of a warm welcome whenever they come home to Newcastle.

Pubs and clubs across Tyneside and beyond will cling to the latest rumours throughout the close season. Should anyone collate a list of alleged transfer targets it may well top a hundred by the time the transfer window closes and of course the club can't sign them all.

Sometimes the players mentioned will simply be being touted by agents to journalists as they are put in the shop window. Occasionally a journo will strike lucky, either by clever guess-work or maybe a useful contact. More often the story will emanate from the pressure of putting something – anything – on the back page.

Every supporter will have their own views on who Rafa should keep and who he should attempt to get rid of. Just because they do not feature in Benitez's plans does not always mean they will move on though. As always the transfer window will contain a long period of the 'dancing around the handbags' stage before the looming deadline forces people to make a move.

Consider last season's summer transfer window, detailed earlier in 'Toon Up'. On the very last day four players departed on loan and one (Christian Atsu) came in on loan, while Moussa Sissoko finally left at the last minute after deciding Tottenham would be his destination.

In all 16 transfers or loan deals were done by Newcastle in the last ten days of the summer window and while it would be great to think that Rafa had his business done by the start of pre-season training, it is pie in the sky to think that will be the case.

With Benitez having been assured he can have, "Every last penny the club generates" to give the Geordie public a team to be proud of, Rafa will look to assemble a team for the Premier League just as he succeeded in creating a squad for the Championship.

"I'm pleased with how the meeting went and the positive approach we are all taking together to build on what we have started this season" commented Rafa following end of season conversations with the club's top brass. Confirming that planning for the future had already been under way before the end of the campaign Benitez added, "There will be challenges ahead of course. The summer will not be easy but the hard work has been going on for some time and we can now continue positively with the development of the squad ahead of the start of the new season."

Having made a profit of around £30m in his transfer dealings during his time at the club Rafa might hope to get his hands on that as well as funds generated through TV money, sponsorship, season ticket sales, merchandise and whatever is raised from player sales.

Whatever the size of Benitez's war-chest there are two things that seem certain. One is that it will be a phenomenal sum of money, more than Newcastle have ever spent before. The second certainty is that although it will be a huge sum to put at the manager's disposal it will be nowhere near as big as that of many other Premier League clubs, and they will all start with squads that were good enough to hold their own in the top flight last season.

What Benitez will see as his priorities for strengthening is open to debate. Everyone will have their own view but with another of Benitez's strengths being his ability to smile politely and answer questions, in fact he rarely gives anything away and is a dab hand at keeping his card close to his chest. This can only be to Newcastle's advantage as he looks to negotiate.

As well as Newcastle did in 2016-17 the plain fact is that they pipped Brighton by one point and a dispassionate look at The Seagulls squad would conclude that they lack sufficient quality to prosper in the Premier League, so where might Newcastle and Benitez think they might need to strengthen?

Of the signings which took the Toon Up the failures were the ones from abroad. Matz Sels lost his place early on, Jesus Gamez started just two league games and Achraf Lazaar was never even named in the starting line-up for a league match. Between them the trio cost an estimated £9m which is small beer by Premier League standards but nonetheless it was money that went largely down the drain, unless any of that trio are about to show that they actually just needed a year to acclimatise to English football and they'll be better next time around. Who knows?

After all, overseas players Mo Diame and DeAndre Yedlin were already used to the English game when they arrived and did much better. Gayle, Ritchie, Clark, Hayden, Atsu, Murphy and to a lesser extent Hanley all made a positive contribution in their first season at the club but none of them had to experience learning to cope with English football, weather food or language.

Whether United take many more players from the continent and in particular France remains to be seen. Benitez is in a position of enormous strength and would appear to have won the right to control signings with the influence of Graham Carr now significantly diminished from his once all powerful status when it came to player recruitment. Nonetheless Carr remains a confidante of Mike Ashley and has extensive contacts particularly throughout France and the Netherlands. If Carr remains a key player behind the scenes much will depend on how Rafa relates to him, and whether Benitez feels that Carr acquiesces with the direction the manager wants to take the team in.

Starting with the goalkeeping position it is highly likely that a new 'keeper will be brought in and if United want to set a standard it would seem that England 'keeper Joe Hart could be an ideal fit. Amazingly not required at Manchester City, Hart has broadened his horizons with a year in Italy with Torino but would surely jump at the chance to come back into the Premier League on a big stage like Newcastle. With the World Cup coming up and more competition for his England shirt than for many a year through Jack Butland, Jordan Pickford, Toon old boy Fraser Forster, Tom Heaton and maybe even Ben Foster, putting the Hart into Newcastle could be a great move for both club and player.

Another option from Serie A might be Pepe Reina. A compatriot of Rafa, he was a great success at Anfield when Benitez signed him for Liverpool. Having also worked with the 'keeper at Napoli, Rafa would have no trouble placing his confidence in the experienced stopper if he could persuade the Spain international to return to these shores.

At full back the competition between Vurnon Anita and DeAndre Yedlin looks good on the right with both players likely to do well in the top flight. However there is no guarantee that the out of contract Anita will be offered a new deal despite his versatility and youth so perhaps a right back could be on the shopping list. Gamez is reaching the veteran stage and would have to do better in the Premier League than at the lower level but given his background maybe that might suit him. Rafa is ruthless though and the chances are he has already decided to give Gamez the chop.

There would always be the option of bringing in a right back in January but it is undoubtedly at left back where Rafa is likely to target a replacement. As well as Paul Dummett has done there he is probably better at centre back while Achraf Lazaar was so far away from pushing to be first choice that it would seem likely he'll either be moved on or loaned out, even if the former Palermo player is content to sit and pick up wages no doubt far in excess of what he earned in Sicily.

A top class centre back may well be at the top of Benitez's wish list. Ciaran Clark was without doubt the best of United's central defenders last season but in his last experience of the Premier League he was part of an Aston Villa side who finished rock bottom. Clark has enjoyed a confidence building fresh start on Tyneside and seems well equipped to hold down one of the two central defensive berths. Hanley seems certain to step back down to the Championship and Mbemba would seem to have failed to sufficiently impress Benitez in the Championship year. The ex-Anderlecht man fared better in his last year in the Premier League although the inescapable fact is that with him as a regular he couldn't prevent the Toon going down.

While Jamaal Lascelles was handed the captaincy ahead of the promotion season it will be intriguing to see if he retains the armband as he may not retain his place. For all his commitment, at times Lascelles wasn't at ease when under pressure, especially if not alongside Clark. Playing against the likes of Chelsea, Spurs and Manchester City Lascelles and co are more likely to find themselves under much more severe pressure than even the best Championship teams could put them, and if one man understands this it will be Benitez. With a Premier League size war-chest burning a hole in his pocket expect him to invest in a defender he can build the team around.

Never afraid to spend big, Benitez's spent around £230m in six years at Liverpool when prices were markedly more modest than they are now. During the same period from 2004-05 until 2009-10 Rafa raked in around £150m from his Anfield sales. When it comes to defenders if he could unearth another Martin Skrtel for United that would give the base of the side an uncompromisingly solid look rather than the soft centre the defence might have if Rafa was tempted to stick with what he has.

In midfield Matt Ritchie and Jonjo Shelvey have what it takes to play in the Premier League although the step up from the Championship mean that they won't have things as much their own way as when they were ripping teams apart as table toppers. The expected confirmation of Christian Atsu's signing brings him into the equation, although as he was used more off the bench than as a starter in the promotion season the Ghana international may find himself primarily employed as an impact sub.

Isaac Hayden impressed and showed plenty of evidence of his Arsenal schooling in his first year at Newcastle. He will hope to be an influential member of the squad in the Premier League although he may well find he is a player regularly rotated by Rafa, as he was for much of last season. Whether that rotation is with Jack Colback is open to question.

Colback is not everyone's cup of tea but he has done well in the Premier League in the past, even earning a call up to an England squad. Benitez knows that if you give the ball away in the Premier League you might not get it back for a while and one thing Colback does do is retain possession. He's good at keeping it moving and re-cycling it around the side, feeding players who can do damage. Killingworth born, Colback will always give his all for the shirt but whether he proves to be part of Benitez's plans only time will tell.

No doubt one or more Premier League quality midfielders will arrive to raise the bar and also the competition for places. This may be the area where United make a marquee signing, although of course they face the difficulty of the fact that such a player would no doubt prefer to go to a club who can offer him European football.

However when Newcastle dropped out of the Premier League, such is the pull of Benitez combined with the size of the club that Matt Ritchie and Mo Diame were prepared to give up a year in the top flight for the chance to get there with the Toon. It is certainly far from impossible that Rafa could convince a player he really wants to come and help Newcastle now with the prospect of qualifying for Europe sooner rather than later. Benitez will have no intention of hanging around to be an also ran and perhaps players will recognise that.

With his days at Old Trafford seemingly numbered if Wayne Rooney wants an astronomical payday he'll follow Papiss Cisse, Demba Ba and

Obafemi Martins – not to mention Didier Drogba and Oscar – into the Chinese Super League. However if he just wants to play football at the top level and fight for a place in England's World Cup squad, St, James' could be the ideal place for a Premier League encore for the Manchester United legend.

As the promotion season started it seemed as if Yoan Gouffran would be on his way. The Frenchman was re-energised in the Championship and made a firm contribution, particularly in the early part of the season. However having turned 31, combined with the fact that he had found it tougher in the Premier League he would seem unlikely to be involved in the next part of the journey. Ten years younger than Gouffran, Rolando Aarons also started the promotion campaign well before injury stopped him in his tracks. In the Premier League pace throughout the side is crucial and pace is the main thing the Jamaican born bolter brings to the table, so providing he can prove his fitness Rolando may well find himself part of the squad and maybe given a year to prove he should remain beyond that.

Of those out on loan while the boys back home were winning the league, should any of them force their way into Benitez's plans it would come as a major shock. In all likelihood the club and their agents will be looking to find new clubs for these players, possibly adding a little to the United kitty as well as getting them off the wage bill.

At any level of football the hardest thing to do is to score. That's the simple reason why good strikers cost a premium price. In the entire season in 2016-17 only five men did what Dwight Gayle did in the Championship by January – which is to score 20 goals. Of that quintet, two of them – Diego Costa and Sergio Aguero – only reached that final tally on the last day of the season. Sanchez, Lukaku and Kane were the three out in front and clearly to sign players of their calibre costs serious money even if they could be persuaded to come to a club not in the Champions League.

Not one of Southampton, Stoke City, West Ham, West Brom, Hull City or Middlesbrough had a player who reached double figures in the goal-scoring charts in 2016-17 which highlights the difficulty of finding the back of the net on a regular basis in the top flight. With Ritchie, Shelvey and hopefully the signing of a goal-scoring midfielder United should have the ability to share goals around and take the weight off the front man because the perfect example of the consequences of not having goals coming from around the side was down the road at The Stadium of Light. No team in the bottom half of the Premier League had a scorer who notched more than the 15 Jermain Defoe managed, but as the rest of the Sunderland squad couldn't equal Defoe's tally between them it was no surprise they propped up the table, 16 points from safety – more than a point behind for every goal Defoe scored.

The need for not simply relying on your striker for goals is doubly important given that most teams, including Newcastle, usually just play with a single striker nowadays. Having a couple of forwards with a dozen goals each in a 4-4-2 formation takes the pressure off the midfield to get on the mark regularly whereas even if your front man bags a creditable 15 that leaves you short if goals aren't coming from elsewhere.

Up front for United Dwight Gayle looks the man from the championship most likely to find the back of the net. It may be a worrying thought to note that in his last season in the Premier League only three of his goals came in league games, and that in his three seasons in the top flight he totalled 15 goals at that level, with seven representing his best campaign.

No doubt Dwight is a better player now and having done so well in taking the Toon Up he will start the season full of confidence. Surely most supporters would back him to register a personal best total of Premier League goals in his first top flight campaign on Tyneside but expecting him to score anywhere near as frequently as he did in the Championship is a big ask. A key factor will be keeping him fully fit so that his natural pace, which is one of his biggest assets, allows him to get into goal-scoring positions.

Of the Toon's other forwards, Ayoze Perez is perhaps even more of an enigma than Mitrovic. Possibly he could be the goal-scoring midfielder who can complement the lone striker and as he will have just turned 24 shortly before the start of the season there is more to come from the man from Tenerife. Under long term contract to 2021, Perez has to prove he is worth a place in a Premier League team by producing an end product on a consistent basis both in terms of goals and assists. The promotion season saw him score double the number of goals he managed in his last year in the Premier League and now as he matures he needs to produce consistently at the higher level if he is to remain in Rafa's thoughts as the team hopefully continue to climb.

Veteran Daryl Murphy was signed for his knack of notching goals in the Championship and made his contribution when called upon. He hasn't played in the English Premier League since 2009-10 when he appeared three times without scoring. He also failed to register in his previous 34 Premier League outings stretching back to his last English Premier League goal in February 2008. At 34 years old it would seem that like Grant Hanley, Murphy will step back to the Championship if he can find a club, although staying as a squad player cannot be ruled out for the likeable Irish international.

While Murphy is coming to the end of his career, Aleksandar Mitrovic has his career stretching ahead of him. The 22 years old Serbia centre-forward divides opinion amongst Toon fans more than any other player. For some he is the classic give it all you've got spearhead they know centre-backs hate playing against, while for others he is a liability.

On his day 'Mitro' can be virtually unplayable. His physical prowess and determination can make him a dynamic and exciting forward. A run of three braces in four games, including a World Cup qualifying game in the autumn, illustrated he can score regularly. In the high octane world of the Premier League there are plenty of defenders who would not relish a show-down with the Serb who managed nine goals in his one Premier League season, even though he was just 21 years of age.

On the other hand, after his successive braces against Preston in the EFL Cup and Championship in October he scored only one more goal for Newcastle all season, the winner at Wolves.

The dilemma over Mitrovic also has to weigh up the fact that he is a young player who is willing to learn but counter-balanced by the enduring question marks concerning his temperament. Newcastle would be foolish to let go a player who may learn to keep his cool more than he did as a younger man – and he wasn't sent off in the promotion season after two red cards the year before. Potentially The Serb could be a feared forward throughout the game if his plus points can be marshalled, his tendency to see the red mist decrease with maturity, and his end product become more consistent.

With just one striker likely to be played and with eight fewer games to contest in the Premier League, competition for the striker's position will be intense. Mitrovic does have the advantage that his style of play offers a distinct Plan B for Benitez as distinct from the Dwight Gayle option and even if Daryl Murphy departs, young Adam Armstrong is still working his way through the ranks.

Ultimately, along with a left back, centre back, midfielder and quite probably a goalkeeper, Benitez will look to bring in a striker. He will know that there is no point signing a half-way decent player. That wouldn't improve the squad, raise the standard or take Gayle to a new level to keep him as the number one attacking option. Bringing in players from abroad is a gamble and one that can backfire as with Rafa's overseas imports ahead of the Championship campaign. However it may be that a big money gamble is needed and with great knowledge and contacts across the continent Rafa may bring in a forward eager to break into English football, either as a final chapter in a stellar career (As Mourhino did with Ibrahimovic) or maybe a striker yet to reach his peak and keen to take on the Premier League challenge…and wages.

Having spent over £50m in readying his squad for the Championship, Rafa may well invest far more than that as he prepares for the Premier League. Possibly though he will bring in fewer new faces but better quality ones.

As always the Toon Army can be Newcastle's twelfth man but with Manchester City and Liverpool having extended their grounds, West Ham moving to the London Stadium and Spurs renting Wembley while their new ground is constructed, St. James' will no longer have one of the top three capacities in the Premier League. The Tyneside citadel will only be the seventh biggest stadium out of 20, itself an indication of how the Premier League is continuing to expand.

Whereas the size of your fan-base was once a major determinant of a club's likely success, in the modern game it is TV riches rather than gate money which dominate the finances of the wealthiest football league in the world. So while there are six stadia bigger than St. James' there are another six which are barely half as big as St. James' with Bournemouth's base barely half that of the second smallest top flight arena.

Rather like the way in which Rafa will be looking for quality over quantity in his summer recruitment the backing that United receive home and away in the Premier League will be the envy of the country. Supporters are not for sale in the transfer window. It is true that some clubs may have more bums on seats than St. James' can hold but how many of those are spectators waiting to be entertained, and how many are supporters ready to really get behind their team is another matter. In the north-east football matters differently to elsewhere. That's not to say other clubs' fans cannot be passionate but by the end of the second season back in the Premier League it will be the 50th anniversary of the last time the Toon won a major trophy and the fans crave success that many others have grown used to. If anyone can end that dismal record it is Rafa Benitez. Every member of the Toon Army realises that and as Rafa leads the Lads into the future the hope is that it will continue to be a case of Toon Up and Up.

WHAT'S IN STORE?

With the fixtures for the new season set to be announced on June 14th and the big kick-off to take place on the weekend of August 12/13 anticipation will reach fever pitch as the countdown to the season approaches.

With the 2018 World Cup in Russia coming up the Premier League will conclude on May 13th 2018 – a week earlier than it did in 2017.

Newcastle have only been away from the Premier League for a year and will look for at least a season of consolidation on their return but what awaits Newcastle and the sides they are promoted with? Take a look at what awaits, in the order they finished in the top flight while Newcastle were winning promotion.

CHELSEA

Champions by eight clear points in 2016-17 Chelsea had no European distractions as they stormed to the title. Antonio Conte enjoyed instant success amongst a stellar cast of top European managers and will be joined in the Premier League by another member of that exclusive club – and ex Chelsea manager – Rafa Benitez! Utilising wing-backs and employing the pace to annihilate teams on the break, Conte got the best out of an already fabulous squad he will refresh in the summer. A serious bet to win the Champions League, the Blues will be the team to beat if anyone wants to take their Premier League crown.

TOTTENHAM HOTSPUR

No team have taken more Premier League points over the last two seasons as Spurs. Mauricio Pochettino's side were so good they finished eight points clear of moneybags Manchester City. Runs of nine and six consecutive Premier League victories would normally be expected to lead a team to the top but Tottenham just couldn't reel in The Blues, a run of four successive draws costing them mid-season momentum when they were distracted with Champions League ties. Spurs struggled playing their European games at Wembley and with Wembley being their temporary home for 2017-18 while work at their newly developed stadium is carried out, Spurs may encounter the sort of difficulties that afflicted West Ham in their first year in a big new open stadium away from the tight confines of the Boleyn Ground. Nonetheless any team featuring two of the brightest young English talents in Harry Kane and Dele Alli will test any opponent and having signed off 2016-17 with stunning 6-1 and 7-1 away wins Spurs have made it clear that they intend to remain a force to be reckoned with.

MANCHESTER CITY

Even the presence of Mourinho, Klopp and Conte couldn't over-shadow Manchester City's acquisition of Pep Guardiola for the start of the 2016-17 season. Just as Rafa Benitez was the biggest boss in the Championship – even though Roberto Di Matteo at Villa meant Rafa was not the only Champions League winner at that level – so Guardiola was heralded as the biggest of the big beasts occupying the Premier league hot-seats. It wasn't until the 11th game of the season that anyone stopped them winning, Celtic holding City to an exciting 3-3 Champions league draw at Parkhead. To general amazement Guardiola didn't see another victory for five more matches as inconsistency became the byword for City's season. Beating Barcelona and only drawing at home to 'Boro seemed to sum them up. 11 times they scored four or more but three times conceded as many when the soft underbelly of their defence was exposed. Guardiola's decision to do without England 'keeper Joe Hart looked like a monumental error. Finishing 15 points off top spot in a trophy-less season will have hurt City but having had a year to get used to the Premier League they will expect to do better and will be another of the sides where taking a point or more from them will be a considerable achievement.

LIVERPOOL

Jurgen Klopp has some way to go to be as successful at Anfield as Rafa Benitez, but in taking the Reds back into the Champions League in his first full season the German is already living up to the hype. Recovering from a lengthy mid-season slump where the only win in 10 was an FA Cup replay against Plymouth, Liverpool lost only one of their last dozen matches. Possessing some outstandingly talented players such as former United man Gini Wijnaldum, talisman Phillipe Coutinho and the ex-Southampton pair Sadio Mane and Adam Lallana, Liverpool can take some taming. However coping with the demands of the Champions League may affect them, especially with the pressing game Klopp likes them to implement. Newcastle v Liverpool matches have produced some classic games and with Rafa up against his old club the fixtures between the clubs will be amongst the tastiest of the season.

ARSENAL

Toon fans may gasp with incredulity at those long suffering Arsenal supporters who under Arsene Wenger have been in three of the last four FA Cup finals, done the double twice, won the Premier League for a third time, won six FA Cups ahead of the 2017 final and qualified for the Champions League in for 20 seasons in a row, reaching the final in 2006. All that and moving to a fabulous new stadium while playing some of the best football witnessed in the modern era. Goodness knows how they've coped and in 2016-17 they had to put up with only finishing fifth, an entire point away from a Champions League place.

Whether Wenger stays, moves 'upstairs' or leaves his love affair with The Gunners only time will tell. If Wenger stays Arsenal will be a possession based team capable of unpicking the tightest defenders. If the North London club elect to go for a change in 2017-18 they might find that they do not have things all their own way – as with Guardiola at Manchester City – or find that a new regime re-energises them so that their supporters no longer have to put up with such lean years...

MANCHESTER UNITED

Jose Mourinho's first season at Old Trafford saw him effectively give up on attempting to qualify for the Champions League via Premier League placing. Instead he put his eggs into the basket marked qualification via the Europa League, where United met Ajax of Amsterdam in the final in Stockholm. It was United's second final under the man who was Sir Bobby Robson's translator at FC Porto, United having already won the League Cup.

The Premier League will be a higher priority for Jose after a full season at Old Trafford. Building a new dynasty to follow on from the golden era under Sir Alex Ferguson is a challenge which Mourinho accepted, and having won the Champions League with Porto and Inter but not with Chelsea or Real Madrid, he won't rest until he has taken Europe's top prize with a third club. After breaking the transfer record to bring in Paul Pogba, Mourinho will spend massively again so that any game with

Manchester United will be as difficult as it always has been for the last half century.

EVERTON

Everton were in a league of their own in 2016-17. Finishing eight points behind sixth placed Manchester United and 15 ahead of eighth placed Southampton, Evertonians rarely got up on a match-day and wondered if they'd climb up or slip down the table. The Toffees have one of the very best crops of young players coming through the ranks at Goodison Park. Having seen Tom Davies follow on from Ross Barkley look out for Dominic Calvert-Lewin, Kieran Dowell, Callum Connolly, Jonjoe Kenny and Ademola Lookman who were team-mates of Adam Armstrong and Freddie Woodman in the England Under 20 squad at the 2017 Under 20 World Cup in South Korea. Under the ambitious Ronald Koeman Everton will once again be a top half team in a Premier League which gets more competitive every year.

SOUTHAMPTON

Unlucky not to win the League Cup in the Wembley final against Manchester United, The Saints eventually just pipped south coast rivals Bournemouth to eighth place on goal difference. In a sign of how far ahead the rest of the Premier League is from the also-rans Southampton had a minus goal difference despite their lofty position and were fully 23 points behind Manchester United just two places above them. In contrast that is just one more point than separated champions Newcastle with eight placed Norwich in the Championship. Sofiane Boufal cost The Saints almost £16m and showed his talent only in glimpses while £14.5m January capture Manolo Gabbiadini scored six goals in his first four games but none in his last eight. It will be a big season for both of those forwards with Saints lack of goals possibly costing them in 2017-18 unless they can keep Charlie Austin fit.

BOURNEMOUTH

How long until the Cherry that is Eddie Howe is picked is the biggest question surrounding a tiny club punching way above their weight. For Bournemouth to finish in the top half and outscore Manchester United is a phenomenal achievement. Whether they can continue to be so successful once Howe is lured away is a matter for debate. Under the country's most talented young manager Bournemouth have been well drilled and considerably more than the sum of their parts. No doubt Matt Ritchie will relish the thought of going up against his old club who to their credit did better in their second season in the Premier League than in their first. The Dorset outfit will look to sustain their upward trajectory but Newcastle will have ambitions of finishing above this club who started the decade in League Two.

WEST BROMWICH ALBION

Of all the teams you would expect to be 'on the beach' early the last one is probably West Brom. Yet Tony Pulis' team took a miserable one point from their last eight games yet still finished in the top half – or 'haaaf' as Pulis would say. The Baggies only dropped two places from the eighth place they were in after beating Arsenal in March but that late season drop off in form might give cause to worry around The Hawthorns, especially as they are one of the clubs in dire need of a regular goal-scorer. Pulis has always been a pragmatic manager and one who can be expected to keep The Baggies out of danger but West Brom is a club The Magpies can look to overtake.

WEST HAM UNITED

The helter-skelter style sculpture you'll see on Newcastle's first visit to West Ham's new ground is emblematic of their opening season at the stadium built for the 2012 Olympics. The Hammers whirled around in dizzyish fashion, lurching from good runs to bad ones as they tried to acclimatise to their new home. Having been used to the close confines of The Boleyn Ground, moving to the Olympic Stadium was like the occupants of The Little Theatre in Gateshead suddenly taking over The Theatre Royal, and they struggled to cope. On five occasions they conceded four or more goals at their new home and Slaven Bilic felt the heat. Having had a season to get used to their new surroundings West Ham might no longer be such a soft touch there. If not then having lost their star man Dimitri Payet since United last played them they could possibly be in trouble.

LEICESTER CITY

The party is over at The Kingpower. Champions as Newcastle went down, Leicester enjoyed their Champions League adventure while United were winning the Championship but sacked kingmaker Claudio Ranieri while they were still competing in Europe. Turning to (Craig) Shakespeare, for a while it was 'All's Well That Ends Well' as The Foxes won six games in a row. Since that spell the only wins in their last 10 were against out of form West Brom and Watford, while they lost 1-6 at home to Spurs in the last week of the season. 2017-18 could be as disappointing for Leicester as their last season in the same league as The Toon was exhilarating.

STOKE CITY

Finishing 13th after three successive ninth place finishes took Stoke back to the same position they managed before they got stuck in ninth. The league was so tight though that had The Potters managed just three more points they would have been eighth! Mark Hughes has assembled a squad that contains talented players such as Xherdan Shaqiri and Marko Arnautovic but will hope his big money buy Saido Berahino can start scoring the goals he was bought to supply. Still a difficult side to play against even though they are more attractive than during the Tony Pulis era, Stoke will probably once again be mid-table material.

CRYSTAL PALACE

Big Sam's brief sojourn with the England team came crashing around his ears but with skin the thickness of a rhinoceros it didn't take Allardyce long to take over from Alan Pardew at Selhurst Park. It took longer to turn Palace around but sensational wins at Chelsea and Liverpool combined with a solid 3-0 home win over Arsenal illustrated that love him or loathe him Sam Allardyce's teams can never be taken lightly. With talented front players at his disposal and a typically Allardyce drilled defence Palace are a team who will survive as long as Big Sam stays but nonetheless the Toon will aim to finish above them.

SWANSEA CITY

Taking over exactly half way through the season Paul Clement inspired the Swans to take 29 points from 19 games. If he could repeat that over a full season The Jacks would be a very comfortable eighth based on the 2016-17 table. Even if the South Wales side manage to hang on to star man Gylfi Sigurdsson no-one will expect them to do that well but they will start the season full of confidence after finishing with four wins and a draw at Old Trafford. Without major investment Swansea may be a side dragged into the danger zone again and are another club who Newcastle will hope to end the campaign looking down on, especially as their porous defence leaked more goals than anyone but Hull last season.

BURNLEY

Media darlings they may be and with good reason as a small club extracting every last drop of potential from a workmanlike team well drilled by Sean Dyche. Burnley like to rough things up a bit though, sailing close to what they can get away with in the modern game. Centre-forward Ashley Barnes is a handful physically while Andre Gray is similar in style to Dwight Gayle, although he is said to have interested Newcastle. At the back Burnley benefit from top goalkeeper Tom Heaton and highly rated centre-back Michael Keane. Their continued survival will hinge on keeping their key players particularly as their much vaunted home form fell away late in the season. After losing at home to then non-league Lincoln in the FA Cup, The Clarets won only one and lost three of their remaining half dozen fixtures at what had previous been an almost impregnable Turf Moor, and they ended up alongside Watford just above the drop zone. United will be disappointed if they aren't above Burnley come the end of the campaign.

WATFORD

In sacking Walter Mazzarri at the end of the season, Watford continued their churn of managers that has seen them dispose of the services of seven bosses since Sean Dyche departed in the summer of 2012. The men from Vicarage Road had 40 points on the board after 32 games but the 'The Golden Boys' evidently then decided to think about their tans as the last six matches were lost, nine goals being conceded in the final two games. Much will depend on whoever takes over as the next incumbent but quite possibly sooner or later Watford will finish in the bottom three.

BRIGHTON & HOVE ALBION

The first manager to lose his job in the Premier League just a few short months after getting Newcastle promoted with over 100 points Chris Hughton will hope to have longer in the top flight with Brighton, although he will understand his squad will require an injection of Premier League quality if it is to survive. Quite possibly the Seagulls will make a good start as so many promoted sides do, but sustaining it over a season may be a big ask and staying in the top flight may represent an even bigger achievement for Hughton than getting them there in the first place.

HUDDERSFIELD TOWN

David Wagner's Huddersfield won penalty shoot-outs in both the final and semi-final of the Play-offs to become the first team to win promotion to the Premier League despite a minus goal difference in the Championship! With what was said to be the fourth smallest budget in the division, Wagner worked wonders to take The Terriers up and will need to work another to enable them to stay up.

Newcastle then will face many more fixtures against well-established quality teams than against sides who might struggle. While it would be wonderful for United to storm the table and end up counting their place from the top rather than the bottom Benitez will have a clear objective. As he took the Toon Up the focus remained firmly on simply winning promotion.

Having achieved that the next step will be a solid one of re-establishing Newcastle United in the Premier League. That won't be easy and one of the keys to success will be in how set-backs are responded to. Rafa will assemble a side to take on the big boys but that might take several transfer windows.

There is just cause for belief in Benitez to keep bringing the good times back to Newcastle. He has already made a brilliant start and as United travel along the roads still to come they should be accompanied by all the smiling faces.

TOON UP TEST

1) Name the four players who debuted in the opening game of the season at Fulham.

2) **Who scored the first Toon goal of the season?**

3) Who were the opponents the first time Dwight Gayle and Matt Ritchie were both on the score-sheet?

4) **Who was the only player to score more than once in the 6-0 win at QPR?**

5) What was the name of Italy's Italia '90 goalkeeper who came to Newcastle as manager of Wolves?

6) **Who were the two teams Dwight Gayle scored hat-tricks against?**

7) Which two players notched a brace against Preston in the EFL Cup?

8) Who scored home and away against Cardiff City?

9) Who scored the winner for Blackburn Rovers in both games against United?

10) Who was the only Toon player to score in the penalty shoot-out at Hull?

11) Against which team did Dwight Gayle register his 20th goal of the season?

12) Who was the 16 year old who scored twice at St. James' for Fulham?

13) Can you name the referee who incorrectly disallowed Matt Ritchie's penalty against Burton Albion?

14) Who scored twice on the night Newcastle mathematically secured promotion against Preston?

15) Who was the Aston Villa player whose late goal against Brighton enabled Newcastle to clinch the Championship trophy?

16) Who was United's Player of the Year?

17) Can you name the three Newcastle players selected in the PFA Championship Team of the Season?

18) Can you name the three players who each scored one goal during the season?

19) Which team was the highest attendance of the season recorded against?

20) How many goals did Newcastle score in all competitions in 2016-17?

ANSWERS

1) Matz Sels, Grant Hanley, Isaac Hayden and Dwight Gayle.

2) Dwight Gayle (Against Huddersfield).

3) Reading

4) Jonjo Shelvey

5) Walter Zenga

6) Norwich City and Birmingham City

7) Aleksandar Mitrovic and Mo Diame.

8) Christian Atsu

9) Charlie Mulgrew

10) Christian Atsu

11) Brentford

12) Ryan Sessegnon

13) Keith Stroud

14) Ayoze Perez

15) Jack Grealish

16) Ciaran Clark

17) Jamaal Lascelles, Jonjo Shelvey and Dwight Gayle.

18) Grant Hanley, Chancel Mbemba and DeAndre Yedlin

19) Leeds United

20) 100

Sky Bet Championship Table

	P	W	D	L	F	A	GD	Pts
Newcastle United	**46**	**29**	**7**	**10**	**85**	**40**	**45**	**94**
Brighton & Hove Albion	46	28	9	9	74	40	34	93
Reading	46	26	7	13	68	64	4	85
Sheffield Wednesday	46	24	9	13	60	45	15	81
Huddersfield Town	46	25	6	15	56	58	-2	81
Fulham	46	22	14	10	85	57	28	80
Leeds United	46	22	9	15	61	47	14	75
Norwich City	46	20	10	16	85	69	16	70
Derby County	46	18	13	15	54	50	4	67
Brentford	46	18	10	18	75	65	10	64
Preston North End	46	16	14	16	64	63	1	62
Cardiff City	46	17	11	18	60	61	-1	62
Aston Villa	46	16	14	16	47	48	-1	62
Barnsley	46	15	13	18	64	67	-3	58
Wolverhampton Wanderers	46	16	10	20	54	58	-4	58
Ipswich Town	46	13	16	17	48	58	-10	55
Bristol City	46	15	9	22	60	66	-6	54
Queens Park Rangers	46	15	8	23	52	66	-14	53
Birmingham City	46	13	14	19	45	64	-19	53
Burton Albion	46	13	13	20	49	63	-14	52
Nottingham Forest	46	14	9	23	62	72	-10	51
Blackburn Rovers	46	12	15	19	53	65	-12	51
Wigan Athletic	46	10	12	24	40	57	-17	42
Rotherham United	46	5	8	33	40	98	-58	23

Newcastle United 2016-17 Appearances

	Total Appearances	League Starts	League Subs	Cups Starts	Cups Subs
Matt Ritchie	48	40	2	4	2
Jonjo Shelvey	48	38	4	5	1
Jamaal Lascelles	47	41	2	3	1
Paul Dummett	46	44	1	1	0
Yoan Gouffran	44	33	5	3	3
Ayoze Perez	41	25	11	2	3
Mo Diame	39	25	10	4	0
Isaac Hayden	37	28	5	2	2
Ciaran Clark	36	34	0	2	0
Karl Darlow	36	34	0	2	0
Dwight Gayle	34	26	6	1	1
Jack Colback	34	24	5	4	1
Christian Atsu	34	15	17	1	1
DeAndre Yedlin	32	21	6	4	1
Vurnon Anita	31	24	3	2	2
Aleksandar Mitrovic	29	11	14	4	0
Daryl Murphy	18	7	8	2	1
Grant Hanley	15	5	5	5	0
Sels Matz	14	9	0	5	0
Chancel Mbemba	13	12	0	1	0
Achraf Lazaar	9	0	4	5	0
Jesus Gamez	7	2	3	2	0
Aarons Rolando	5	1	3	1	0
Sammy Ameobi	4	0	4	0	0
Rob Elliott	3	3	0	0	0
Cheick Tiote	3	0	1	2	0
Jamie Sterry	3	0	2	1	0
Massadio Haidara	3	0	1	2	0
Daryl Janmmat	2	2	0	0	0
Adam Armstrong	2	0	2	0	0
Daniel Barlaser	2	0	0	2	0
Yasin Ben El-Mhanni	2	0	0	2	0
Stuart Findlay	1	0	0	1	0

Newcastle United 2016-17 Goal Scorers

	Total	League	Cups
Dwight Gayle	23	23	0
Matt Ritchie	16	12	4
Ayoze Perez	12	9	3
Yoan Gouffran	7	5	2
Mo Diame	6	3	3
Aleksandar Mitrovic	6	4	2
Daryl Murphy	6	5	1
Christian Atsu	5	5	0
Jonjo Shelvey	5	5	0
Ciaran Clark	3	3	0
Jamaal Lascelles	3	3	0
Isaac Hayden	2	2	0
Vurnon Anita	1	1	0
Hanley Grant	1	1	0
Chancel Mbemba	1	1	0
DeAndre Yedlin	1	1	0
Own Goals	3	0	3

Championship 2016-17 Goal Scorers

Chris Wood	27	Leeds United
Dwight Gayle	**23**	**Newcastle United**
Glenn Murray	23	Brighton & HA
Tammy Abraham	23	Bristol City
Jonathan Kodjia	19	Aston Villa / Bristol City
Yann Kermorgant	18	Reading
Cameron Jerome	16	Norwich City
Anthony Knockaert	15	Brighton &HA
Lasse Vibe	15	Brentford
Scott Hogan	15	Aston Villa / Brentford

* League goals only. Not including Cups or Play-offs.

Newcastle United 2016-17 Average Attendances

Newcastle United	**51,111**
Aston Villa	31,901
Derby County	29,104
Brighton & HA	27,619
Leeds United	26,779
Sheffield Wednesday	26,580
Norwich City	26,272
Wolverhampton Wanderers	21,944
Huddersfield Town	20,343
Nottingham Forest	19,207
Bristol City	18,953
Fulham	18,665
Birmingham City	18,137
Reading	17,280
Ipswich Town	16,555
Cardiff City	16,335
Queens Park Rangers	14,426
Barnsley	13,843
Preston North End	12,888
Blackburn Rovers	11,853
Wigan Athletic	11,540
Brentford	10,288
Rotherham United	9,786
Burton Albion	5,078

Instant Promotions

How relegated teams have fared in their first attempt to win promotion.
Promoted teams in bold.

Season Relegated	Club	Position in first season
2015-16	**Newcastle United**	**1**
2015-16	Norwich City	8
2015-16	Aston Villa	13
2014-15	Hull City	4
2014-15	**Burnley**	**1**
2014-15	Queens Park Rangers	12
2013-14	**Norwich City**	**3**
2013-14	Fulham	17
2013-14	Cardiff City	11
2012-13	Wigan Athletic	5
2012-13	Reading	7
2012-13	**Queens Park Rangers**	**4**
2011-12	Bolton Wanderers	7
2011-12	Blackburn	17
2011-12	Wolverhampton Wanderers	23
2010-11	Birmingham City	4
2010-11	Blackpool	5
2010-11	**West Ham United**	**3**
2009-10	Burnley	8
2009-10	Hull City	11
2009-10	Portsmouth	16
2008-09	**Newcastle United**	**1**
2008-09	Middlesbrough	11
2008-09	**West Bromwich Albion**	**2**
2007-08	Reading	4
2007-08	**Birmingham City**	**2**
2007-08	Derby County	18
2006-07	Sheffield Utd	9
2006-07	Charlton	11
2006-07	Watford	6